lonely planet

Diving & Snorkeling
Dominica

Michael Lawrence

LONELY PLANET PUBLICATIONS
Melbourne • Oakland • London • Paris

Diving & Snorkeling Dominica
- A Lonely Planet Pisces Book

1st Edition
September, 1999

Published by
Lonely Planet Publications
192 Burwood Road, Hawthorn, Victoria 3122, Australia

Other offices
150 Linden Street, Oakland, California 94607, USA
10A Spring Place, London NW5 3BH, UK
1 rue du Dahomey, 75011 Paris, France

Photographs
by Michael Lawrence

Front cover photograph
Dominica reef scene
by Michael Lawrence

Back cover photographs
Red-banded lobster, Roseau building with passerby,
diver at Pointe Guignard
by Michael Lawrence

All of the images in this guide are available for licensing
from **Lonely Planet Images**
email:lpi@lonelyplanet.com.au

ISBN 0 86442 764 6

text & maps © Lonely Planet 1999
photographs © photographers as indicated 1999
dive site maps are Transverse Mercator projection

Printed by H&Y Printing Ltd., Hong Kong

Contents

Mid-Island Dive Sites   68

Northern Dive Sites   80

Marine Life   94

Diving Conservation & Awareness   101

Listings   103

Index   106

Author

Michael Lawrence

Michael Lawrence's life has been a twisting, turning path of wildly divergent careers. He was a professional musician for nearly 25 years, playing jazz guitar, doing studio and orchestral work, stage shows, arranging and conducting and doing anything possible to turn jazz pennies into real dollars. A gig on a cruise ship in the Caribbean allowed him his first opportunity to view the underwater world, an experience that soon changed his life. He has written and illustrated well over 300 articles for almost every North American dive publication as well as various publications in South America and Europe. His photos, both underwater and topside, have been published internationally in magazines, calendars, textbooks and advertisements for a variety of industries. Michael considers Dominica to be at the very peak of Caribbean destinations, both for its extraordinary marine environment and for its striking topside attractions.

ROB WATERFIELD

From the Author

For maps, dive site information, dive services and a general check for accuracy, appreciation goes to Michael and Michelle Salzer of Cabrits Dive Center for exploring and detailing the northern sector, Gunther Glatz of East Caribe Dive for his aid in the mid-island section, Arun (Izzy) Madisetti, both for his invaluable help in detailing maps as well as for his personal analysis of the Soufriere crater dive sites and Billy Lawrence of Dive Dominica for his confirmation and expansion of dive site details. Inland, Michael would have been unable to complete his land explorations without the aid of George Ken Dill and his guides (especially Clem James) of Ken's Hinterland Adventure Tours-KHATTS. Mark Melrose has been instrumental in the author's discovery of the island; a better traveling companion could not be found. Thanks for all the U/W modeling, companionship, humor and hang time.

Above all, Michael Lawrence thanks his friends Derek and Ginette Perryman of Dive Dominica and Castle Comfort Dive Lodge for their unflagging friendship and support (along with gallons of rum punch, *ti ponche* and late-night Kabuli). Derek Perryman, the acknowledged architect of Dominican diving, explored these waters, mapped the first series of dive sites, trained the first local divemasters and instructors and single-handedly worked to bring the glories of Dominica, both under and above the water, to the attention of the world. All visiting divers owe him a large debt of gratitude.

Photography Notes

Michael Lawrence uses Nikon cameras for both underwater and land shooting. Underwater, he uses Nikon 8008s, N90s and F4 cameras in Aquatica housings, using 16mm, 18mm, 20mm, 24mm, 60mm and 105mm lenses. For big animals, strong currents and fast action he prefers Nikonos III and V bodies, Sekonic light meters and 15mm lenses along with 28mm and 35mm lenses and various extension tubes for some of his macro work. His strobes of choice are Ikelite 150s and 200s. On land, he uses Nikon N90s and F5 cameras with a full array of lenses. The vast majority of images in this volume were shot on Fuji Velvia and Provia, but he also carries Kodachrome 25 and 64 (when there's time to wait for processing), Ektachrome 100SW and Ektachrome 200SW for low-light situations.

From the Publisher

This first edition was produced in Lonely Planet's U.S. office under direction from Roslyn Bullas, the Pisces Books publishing manager. Wendy Smith edited this book with invaluable contributions from Debra Miller and Sarah Hawkins. Emily Douglas designed the book and cover. Patrick Bock, Roisin O'Dwyer and Chris Whinihan created the maps, which were adapted from the author's comprehensive base maps, under the supervision of Senior Cartographer Alex Guilbert. Bill Alevizon reviewed the Marine Life sections for scientific accuracy.

Lonely Planet Pisces Books

Lonely Planet acquired the Pisces line of diving and snorkeling books in 1997. This series is being developed and substantially revamped over the next few years. We invite your comments and suggestions.

Pisces Pre-Dive Safety Guidelines

Before embarking on a scuba-diving, skin-diving or snorkeling trip, careful consideration should be given to a safe as well as enjoyable experience. You should:

- Possess a current diving certification card from a recognized scuba diving instructional agency (if scuba diving)
- Be sure you are healthy and feel comfortable diving
- Obtain reliable information about physical and environmental conditions at the dive site (e.g. from a reputable local dive operation)
- Be aware of local laws, regulations and etiquette about marine life and environment
- Dive at sites within your experience level; if available, engage the services of a competent, professionally trained dive instructor or dive master

Underwater conditions vary significantly from one region, or even site, to another. Seasonal changes can significantly alter any site and dive conditions. These differences influence the way divers dress for a dive and what diving techniques they use.

Regardless of location, there are special requirements for diving in that area. Before your dive, ask about the environmental characteristics that can affect your diving and how trained local divers deal with these considerations.

Warning & Request

Even with reliable dive guides, things change—dive site conditions, regulations, topside information. Nothing stays the same for long. Your feedback on this book will be used to update future editions and help make the next edition more accurate and useful. Excerpts from your correspondence may appear in our newsletter, Planet Talk, or in the Postcards section of our web site, so please let us know if you don't want your letter published or your name acknowledged.

Correspondence can be addressed to:
Lonely Planet Publications
Pisces Books
150 Linden Street
Oakland, CA 94607
e-mail: pisces@lonelyplanet.com

Introduction

The Natural Queen of the Caribbean, Dominica (pronounced dom-en-EE-ka) is home to some of the highest peaks of the Lesser Antilles and the largest oceanic rainforest in the Caribbean. Dominica appeals to travelers seeking magnificent diving and snorkeling and an authentic, unpretentious West Indian experience.

Visitors come to Dominica not only for the diving—which is indisputably world-class—but also to explore the island's wealth of topside activities. Unlike the flat limestone islands of many Caribbean dive destinations, Dominica is mountainous and verdant. Waterfalls and hot springs nestled in the interior beckon adventurous hikers. Mountain biking and kayaking allow further exploration of the island's land and sea contours. Dominica is also considered one of the finest areas in the Caribbean for whale and dolphin sightings, so organized whale-watching trips have become a standard part of any visitor's agenda.

The underwater terrain is composed of shallow coral patches, sharp pinnacles and sloping and vertical walls interspersed with caverns and swim-throughs. While

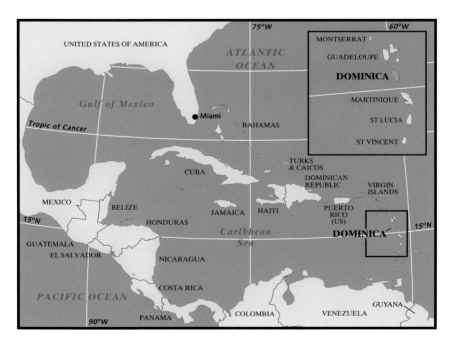

corals are limited to only perhaps two dozen species, the variety of fish and invertebrate life is extraordinary. Many fish considered rare in other destinations—frogfish, seahorses, batfish, pipefish, flying gurnards and more—are seen here regularly. Another of Dominica's outstanding strengths is the variety of sponge formations. Convoluted and large, they are often decorated with crinoids standing on their edges, behavior unusual in most of the Caribbean.

In Dominica, you'll find a West Indian community much as they used to be, relatively unaffected by today's fast-moving, high-tech global community. It is a true working Caribbean island and, as such, shares many of the ills that plague neighboring islands—poverty, drug and alcohol abuse, petty crime, race and class divisions and ecological degradation are concerns for Dominicans inasmuch as they are concerns for all Caribbeans. That said, many of these problems are less pronounced in Dominica and the general atmosphere is very friendly and open. The rich West Indian experience will appeal to dedicated travelers who prefer to avoid big hotels, crowds of people, extravagant entertainment and mindless nightlife. Dominica is a destination for the person seeking the essence of tropical life.

The 41 dive sites covered in this book have been divided into three regional categories: Southern Dive Sites, Mid-Island Dive Sites, and Northern Dive Sites. Information about location, depth range, access and expertise rating is provided for each site. You'll also find detailed descriptions of each site, outlining conditions and noting walls, reefs, caves and the marine life you can expect to see. The Marine Life section provides a gallery of Dominica's common fish and invertebrate life. Though this book is not meant to be a stand-alone travel guide, the Practicalities and Overview sections offer useful information about the island, while the Activities & Attractions section provides descriptions of popular hikes and other topside activities.

Excellent dive sites surround Scotts Head, which forms the south end of Soufriere Bay.

Overview

Many people confuse Dominica with the Dominican Republic, the country that shares the island of Hispaniola with Haiti. Dominica is an island in the West Indies, the 2,500-mile (4,000km) archipelago that arches from Florida to Venezuela. North of Martinique and south of Guadeloupe, Dominica is part of the Lesser Antilles, the chain of islands separating the Caribbean Sea from the Atlantic Ocean.

The vast majority of Dominicans live in small towns and villages along the coast. Many of these are small fishing villages. Dominica's west coast is the leeward side of the island and is protected from harsh weather conditions. As a result, the west coast is more developed with homes, hotels and services for locals as well as visitors. The larger towns are located on the west coast—Roseau, the capital, to the south and Portsmouth to the north. Though less developed, the east coast is home to numerous small villages and the Carib Territory to the northeast. Settlements also exist in the interior, but the difficult terrain and the large areas of protected land mean fewer than along the coast.

Geography

The tallest island in the Eastern Caribbean, Dominica reaches a peak of 4,747ft (1,424m) at Morne Diablotin. The island is 29 miles (47km) long, 16 miles (26km)

Though restricted in certain areas, fishing is still the mainstay of most Dominican villages.

11

wide and has a land mass of 290 sq miles (467 sq km). Dominica is part of what could be called the Caribbean "Rim of Fire," islands born of violent volcanic eruptions. Millions of years ago, fiery forces formed subsea mountains, which gradually rose from the depths to emerge into the light of day. These mountains form the island's intensely rugged terrain—there is evidence of at least a dozen distinct volcanoes and volcanic shafts on the island.

Though it has been more than a century since Dominica has experienced an actual volcanic eruption, the island's still-boiling heart is evident in many ways. Fumaroles—vents leading to molten lava lying below the surface—belch hot gases. Hot springs throughout the island create soothing natural hot tubs.

The Caribbean "Rim of Fire"

Though Dominica hasn't experienced a major volcanic event since 1880—when an eruption from the Morne Trois Pitons area spewed a cloud of volcanic ash over the capital—the volcanic action in the region is far from over. Minor volcanic disturbances are commonly observed by geologists but the most vivid current example of the area's volatility is in Montserrat, where recent eruptions have garnered international attention. The following is a list of major volcanic events in the Eastern Caribbean during the 20th century:

Gas vents in the Valley of Desolation.

1902, St. Vincent: On May 7, La Soufrière volcano erupted, killing some 2,000 people. The eruption created a water-filled crater similar to Dominica's Boiling Lake.

1902, Martinique: On May 8, one day after the St. Vincent event, Mont Pelée erupted. Nearly 30,000 people were killed when the city of Saint-Pierre was wiped out by an ash flow moving at an estimated 100mph. The Mont Pelée eruption is considered the most devastating natural disaster in Caribbean history and the world's third most deadly volcanic eruption since AD 1500. Remarkably, one man—a prisoner in a poorly ventilated, dungeon-like jail cell—survived the eruption.

1976-7, Guadeloupe: Violent activity of La Soufrière volcano in July and August of 1976 caused the evacuation of 73,000 people. Renewed activity in April 1977 again forced thousands from their homes.

1979: St. Vincent: La Soufrière eruptions over ten days in April caused the evacuation of the northern two-thirds of the island.

1995-present, Montserrat: After 400 years of dormancy, the Soufriere Hills volcano began erupting on July 18, 1995, causing the long-term evacuation of the capital and surrounding areas. A major eruption on June 25, 1997 killed 20 people and further reduced the habitable area of the island. All told, the volcanic activity has forced the evacuation of some 8,000 of Montserrat's 12,000 residents.

Morne Trois Pitons is home to the world's second largest solfatara—an exposed, water-filled volcanic crater referred to as the Boiling Lake. The lake's mood changes from day to day, ranging from a low simmer to an outright steaming, gas-belching boil. Offshore, submerged gas vents send bubbles glinting to the surface.

Knitting a seine net for fishing.

Dominica's interior is a jumble of sharp, intersecting angles. The mountains, which act as a magnet for the near-daily rains, serve as the water source for more than 350 rivers that run down the mountain valleys. En route, many of the rivers cascade over steep cliff faces, giving the island an abundance of waterfalls. The rugged terrain makes road construction impossible in many areas, so access to much of the interior is limited to footpaths cutting through thick, quiet greenery.

Beneath the ocean's surface, the terrain reflects that on land. The cliffs that slip into the sea continue their fall below the waterline, so the subsea terrain tends to be angular, with rocky seamounts rising from the depths in severely angled pinnacles.

In Soufriere Bay, dive sites surround a massive submerged caldera—an ancient volcanic crater. Lava flowing from volcanic eruptions created submerged pinnacles—some stretching to within mere feet of the surface—now entirely encrusted with corals, sponges and other invertebrates. The center of the crater reaches depths exceeding 2,000ft (600m). To the west, the waters fall to the extreme depths of the Caribbean Sea.

History

Dominica's early occupants included the Taino branch of the Arawak tribe of South American Indians, a peaceful community of agriculturists, fishermen and hunters who arrived in the Eastern Caribbean about 2,000 years ago.

Sometime around AD 1200 the Carib Indians, a group of warlike tribes also from South America, invaded and eventually took

A tribute to absent fishermen.

over most of the islands of the Caribbean, the sea that bears their name. The Caribs called Dominica Wai'tikibuli, which translates loosely to "tall is her body."

Christopher Columbus first documented Dominica on November 3, 1493 during his second voyage to the New World. Daunted by fierce Carib resistance and discouraged by the lack of gold, the Spanish took little interest in colonizing the island. As it turned out, Dominica was to be the last stand and the final regional stronghold of the Caribs.

Throughout the 17th and 18th centuries, the French and British wrestled over control of Dominica, each country taking and losing the island several times. By 1805, the British gained firm control, utilizing it primarily for sugar production on the lower, more accessible slopes.

As in other Caribbean nations, sugar plantations were worked by massive numbers of West African slaves. The slave trade was vast and brutally inhumane. The Caribbean accounted for nearly 4 million of the New World's 10 million slave importations—a figure that doesn't account for the countless millions who died on slave ships during the voyage. Slavery was eventually outlawed on British islands in 1833. Today, some 95% of Dominica's population is of African descent.

In 1902, after more than 150 years of shadowy existence in the rainforest, the Carib Indians were granted a 3,700-acre (1,500-hectare) tract of land in the northeast now known as the Carib Territory. Today, Dominica is home to some 3,000 native Caribs, the largest true Carib tribe and culture in the Caribbean.

Dominica achieved independence in 1978 and is currently designated as a republic within the British Commonwealth. Today, Dominica displays a mélange of the cultures that have inhabited its shores. Built on a base of African and Amerindian culture and beliefs, a logical British framework overlays an emotional French soul. The French attitude finds expression in the subtle nuances of the local cuisine and in the names of towns and villages. The British colonial power helps things to run properly, creating a workable infrastructure. The result is a fascinating view of true West Indian culture.

The classic silhouette of a tall ship anchored off the coast recalls Dominica's colonial history.

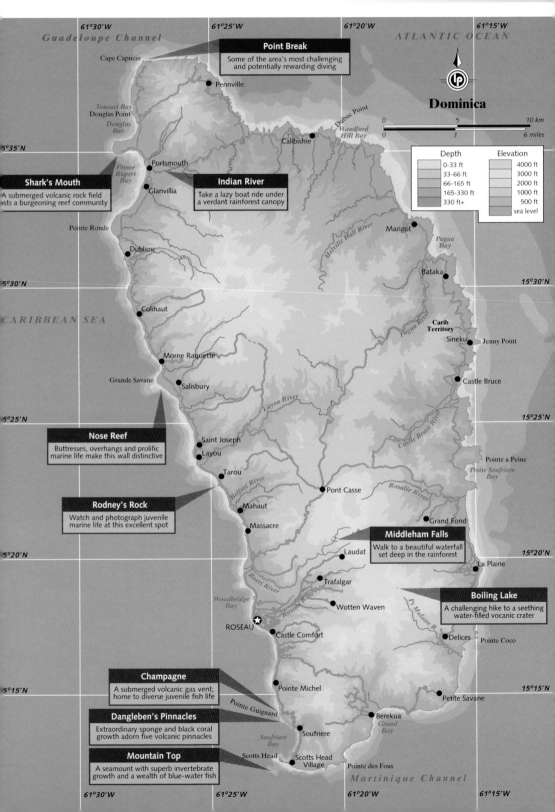

Guadeloupe Channel

ATLANTIC OCEAN

61°30'W · 61°25'W · 61°20'W · 61°15'W

Point Break
Some of the area's most challenging and potentially rewarding diving

Cape Capucin

LP

Dominica

Pennville

Toucari Bay
Douglas Point
Douglas Bay

Dubuc Point
Woodford Hill Bay

5°35'N

Calibishie

0   5   10 km
0   3   6 miles

Portsmouth

Prince Rupert Bay

Depth | **Elevation**

0-33 ft | 4000 ft
33-66 ft | 3000 ft
66-165 ft | 2000 ft
165-330 ft | 1000 ft
330 ft+ | 500 ft
| sea level

Shark's Mouth
A submerged volcanic rock field osts a burgeoning reef community

Glanvillia

Indian River
Take a lazy boat ride under a verdant rainforest canopy

Marigot

Pagua Bay

Pointe Ronde

Dublanc

Melville Hall River

Bataka

5°30'N

15°30'N

Colihaut

Pagua River

Carib Territory

Sineku

Jenny Point

CARIBBEAN SEA

Morne Raquette

Castle Bruce

Grande Savane

Salisbury

Layou River

Castle Bruce River

5°25'N

15°25'N

Nose Reef
Buttresses, overhangs and prolific marine life make this wall distinctive

Saint Joseph

Layou

Belfast River

Tarou

Pont Casse

Rosalie River

Pointe a Peine
Petite Soufriere Bay

Rodney's Rock
Watch and photograph juvenile marine life at this excellent spot

Mahaut

Massacre

Grand Fond

Middleham Falls
Walk to a beautiful waterfall set deep in the rainforest

5°20'N

Laudat

La Plaine

15°20'N

Boeri River

Trafalgar

Rosalie R.

Pt Mulatre R.

Boiling Lake
A challenging hike to a seething water-filled vocanic crater

Woodbridge Bay

Wotten Waven

ROSEAU ☆

Castle Comfort

Delices

Pointe Coco

Champagne
A submerged volcanic gas vent; home to diverse juvenile fish life

Pointe Michel

5°15'N

Petite Savane

15°15'N

Dangleben's Pinnacles
Extraordinary sponge and black coral growth adorn five volcanic pinnacles

Pointe Guignard

Berekua

Grand Bay

Soufriere

Mountain Top
A seamount with superb invertebrate growth and a wealth of blue-water fish

Soufriere Bay

Scotts Head

Scotts Head Village

Pointe des Fous

61°30'W · 61°25'W · 61°20'W · 61°15'W

Martinique Channel

Practicalities

Climate

Dominica enjoys a moderate tropical climate and temperatures vary little throughout the year. January has average highs of 85°F (29°C) and average lows of 68°F (20°C). In July, highs average 90°F (32°C) and lows average 72°F (22°C). Water temperatures, even in the winter, seldom get lower than 76°F (25°C) and average 82°F (27°C) in the summer. Rain is a near-daily affair with February to June being the driest months. You should expect light, refreshing showers several times daily. These statistics apply to the coast; in the hills, expect conditions to be both cooler and wetter. Also be aware that Dominica sits in the Caribbean's hurricane belt—the high season occurs from late August through early October.

Language

English is the primary language. A local language—a colorful creole patois made up of French, African, English and Amerindian words and phrases—is also spoken by many islanders.

Getting There

There are two airports on Dominica. Canefield, north of Roseau on the west coast, serves smaller propeller planes. Melville Hall, on the northwest corner of the island, services jets and larger planes. Though farther from most west coast hotels and guest houses, Melville Hall has taken over as the primary entrance portal, in part because it is the only flat area of land large enough to handle jets.

Diving & Flying

Divers in Dominica usually get there by plane. While it's fine to dive soon *after* flying, it's important to remember that your last dive should be completed at least 12 hours (some experts advise 24 hours) *before* your flight to minimize the risk of residual nitrogen in the blood, which can cause decompression injury.

There are no direct international flights into Dominica. Travelers must fly to a nearby gateway island such as Antigua, Barbados, Guadeloupe, Martinique, Puerto Rico, St. Lucia or St. Martin, and transfer to American Eagle or a regional carrier such as Air Guadeloupe, LIAT or Cardinal Airlines. For those island-hopping in the southeastern Caribbean, the Guadeloupe–Martinique ferry stops in Dominica several times a week. Also, weekly ferries connect Dominica to St. Lucia.

Getting Around

Getting around on the island rarely presents a problem. There are plenty of local and international car-rental agencies and a large fleet of taxis. In addition, you can use the private minivans, occasionally colorfully painted, that function as public buses. They are very inexpensive and relatively convenient. You can flag them down from the road; look for license plates with an *H* or *HA* as a prefix.

Sea creatures with sunglasses adorn a minivan.

Driving in Dominica can be dangerous. If you are not accustomed to difficult mountain roads, driving may be best left to the professionals. As in much of the Caribbean, driving is on the left side of the road (with both left- and right-hand-drive vehicles). Additionally, the roads themselves—with hairpin turns and 180-degree switchbacks on roads barely wide enough for one vehicle—can be frightening. If you choose to drive, be extremely cautious.

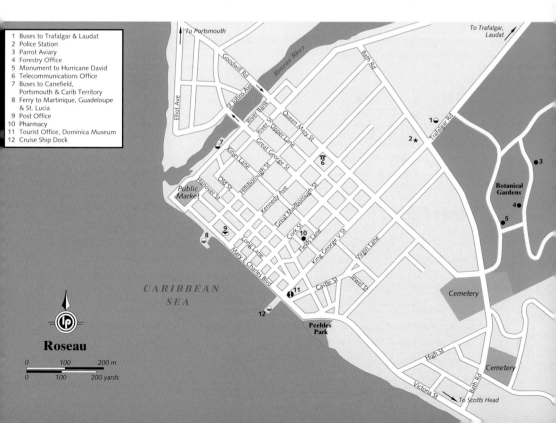

1 Buses to Trafalgar & Laudat
2 Police Station
3 Parrot Aviary
4 Forestry Office
5 Monument to Hurricane David
6 Telecommunications Office
7 Buses to Canefield,
   Portsmouth & Carib Territory
8 Ferry to Martinique, Guadeloupe
   & St. Lucia
9 Post Office
10 Pharmacy
11 Tourist Office, Dominica Museum
12 Cruise Ship Dock

Roseau

Entry

Most visitors to Dominica must have a passport, but U.S. and Canadian citizens may enter with proof of citizenship, such as a voter's identification card or a birth certificate, in conjunction with a valid photo ID. French nationals may enter for up to two weeks with a Carte d'Indentité. Citizens of some Eastern European countries will need visas. A return or ongoing ticket is required of every foreign visitor.

Money

The local currency is the Eastern Caribbean dollar (EC$). This currency, which is shared with several other islands, is fixed to the U.S. dollar and is officially exchanged at the rate of EC$2.67 to US$1. U.S. dollars and international traveler's checks are accepted at major establishments. Many larger professional establishments (including hotels, dive and tour operators, restaurants and car rental agencies) accept Visa, MasterCard and/or American Express. In all cases, it is best to check in advance.

Time

Dominica is on Atlantic Standard Time, which is one hour ahead of Eastern Standard Time and four hours behind GMT. When it's noon on Dominica, it is 4pm in London, 8am in San Francisco, and 1am the following day in Sydney. Daylight saving time is not observed.

Electricity

Electricity on Dominica runs at 220/240 volts at 50 cycles, thus requiring a transformer and adapter plug for appliances using the 110-volt/60-cycle system standard in the U.S. and Canada. Some dive operators and hotels have voltage-stabilized and transformed lines for charging lights and strobes, but you should check in advance. Plugs are European-style: three round prongs in an equilateral triangle or three flat-bladed prongs in the same configuration. The best choice for the traveling diver is to bring an international set of electrical adapters.

Weights & Measures

Dominica uses the imperial system; weight is measured in pounds and ounces, length in feet and inches, distance in miles and temperature in degrees Fahrenheit. Both imperial and metric measurements are used throughout this book except for specific references within a dive site or hike description, which are given in feet and miles.

What to Bring

General supplies are available, though high-quality batteries and other necessities can be difficult to find. Dress is very relaxed with shorts and T-shirts or casual short-sleeved shirts being the norm. Dress is casual at even the finest restaurants, though men should bring a pair of lightweight slacks and women may want to bring a casual dress. Skimpy clothing is not considered acceptable in town.

For diving, you will want to bring a dive skin or light wetsuit for protection from sunburn, coral cuts, stings and other marine hazards as well as for warmth. A 3mm wetsuit should be more than sufficient for Dominica's warm waters. Repair facilities for dive equipment are fairly good though unusual parts will be hard to get. Though sales of dive gear are minimal, most shops have more than enough rental gear should you have problems with your own.

Underwater Photography

Both underwater and topside photo services are minimal. Two photo centers—Depex and Photoworld, both in Roseau—offer C-41 and E-6 processing in addition to other photographic sales and services. However, the processing services are not always dependable and are not recommended for the serious photographer expecting top-quality processing. For casual

A sponge trimmed with crinoids is a willing subject.

Two strobes allow for maxium light control.

snapshots or for underwater photographers anxious to see their images as soon as possible, they will do just fine.

Dive operations in Dominica are just beginning to offer custom underwater photo and video services and classes in underwater photography, but this is still in the first stages of development. You should bring all the film and batteries you think you may need (plus a bit extra) rather than expect to find fresh supplies on the island. Also, make it a point to check that your equipment is in working order before leaving home—it could mean the difference between bringing home the beautiful photographs you want and coming up empty-handed.

Photography Tips

From cultural events to rainforest animals to underwater seascapes, Dominica presents many impressive photographic opportunities. Whether your passion is land or underwater photography, a few specific tips can help you get the shots you're looking for.

On land, use fast wide-angle lenses (at least 28mm) that allow plenty of light penetration. Slower lenses require steady and firm support. Use a monopod or tripod that is light enough to carry on a hike, or rest your camera on a tree root or trunk using a folded shirt or towel to absorb vibrations and keep it from slipping.

Waterfalls shots can be particularly challenging. The secret to a silky professional look is a long exposure, using shutter speeds of ½–2 seconds. (At these slower speeds, you'll definitely need some form of camera support.) Also, try shooting waterfalls in shadow and/or with a smaller f-stop. This evens out exposure latitude and allows for those longer shutter times.

For underwater shots, the secret is using the right tool for the job. For macro work, you'll need extension tubes and close-up kits for amphibious-type systems or 60mm and 105mm lenses for housed SLR cameras. Single strobes will work, but double strobes give added control of light and shadows. If you're using extension tubes or close-up kits and framers, be especially careful not to damage your subject or the environment. Also, never move your macro subject from one location to another. Not only might you harm or stress your subject, you might make it vulnerable to predators.

For underwater wide-angle shots, your greatest impediment will be the density of planktonic life and organic sediment in the water. Here, the secret is strobe control. If you don't light the particles, you won't see them, so use oblique angles and avoid lighting the water between you and your subject. To avoid backscatter, aim your strobes so the inner edge of the light beam hits the subject.

Good luck and good shooting!

Business Hours

Typically, businesses are open Monday through Friday 8am to 1pm and 2 to 4pm, though schedules vary from shop to shop. Many shops are open on weekends, but hours and days vary.

Accommodations

Dominica offers a wide variety of accommodations, from small hotels to intimate rainforest retreats to comfortable bed-and-breakfast–style guest houses. While most hotels can be found along the west coast, there are also some unique establishments found in the interior. Virtually all accommodations are small and locally run, providing highly personalized service. Less expensive rooms are available in informal guest houses. You will not find large commercial resort hotels anywhere on the island. Even Dominica's most upscale hotels tend to be small but very elegant guest houses and cottages.

Proper research can help satisfy your specific tastes. In addition to the established dive resorts and beach hotels, Dominica has many excellent two- to eight-room hotels tucked away in the shadows of the rainforest or along the coast. Many of these are run by expatriates who take pride in providing comfortable and unique accommodations to discerning international travelers. The smallest, most obscure guest house may be operated by a gourmet chef or a superb artist whose talents add to the property's ambiance. A number of

The rugged interior has few residents, so Dominica's mountain retreats offer a true escape.

The Rum Shop: A West Indian Convenience Store

The rum shop is a West Indian tradition, particularly in the southeastern Caribbean. Typically, a rum shop is a tiny, family-run catchall store with loose hours and a friendly, homey atmosphere.

The items offered for sale vary, but usually include basic household necessities, snacks and spirits—often featuring the proprietor's personal rum punch. The food—Caribbean comfort foods like fried chicken and fish—is very inexpensive and is served in a most informal fashion. Perhaps most importantly, the rum shop is a great place to listen in on local gossip and politics and absorb the local lingo.

mountain and rainforest retreats offer a distinctive version of Dominican hospitality. These hotels range from rustic to elegant, but all offer the opportunity to experience the natural environment up close.

Dominica has a number of dive-oriented hotels located all along the west coast. Most dive operators, even ones located on the property of a dedicated dive hotel, offer packages with a choice of accommodations. The style and variety of dive packages vary widely and options change frequently. Some shops will provide transportation between the dive shop and affiliated hotels. If transportation is not available, divers staying in the interior will have to rent a car or do taxi or mini-bus transfers. Most dive boats depart the dock around 8:30 or 9am. See the Listings section for specific information.

Dining & Food

Dominica's cuisine reflects a combination of cultural influences. African, French, East Indian and native flavors are fused into a solid creole style built around the wide variety of spices and produce available on the island. Fresh seafood and produce—including a broad variety of exotic fruits and fruit juices—are

An accordionist adds ambiance to a hotel patio.

Enjoy local fruits and flowers fresh or in sauces, jams and aromatic soaps and lotions.

standouts. Dominica's tap water is safe to drink and the conditions in most restaurants are sanitary.

There are numerous local dining options. You can find anything from inexpensive and tasty meals of fried chicken or fish to truly gourmet dining. Each place has its own unique feeling and all menus feature distinctly Dominican flavors. The hotel restaurants tend to have more conservative service and cuisine, while more casual establishments often serve meals family-style, passing around bowls of vegetables and platters of main dishes.

When you look at a menu featuring local dishes, don't be afraid to ask what the names mean. They can be confusing as many are either local terms or foreign names with local connotations. Dominica's national dish, for example, is "mountain chicken," which is not made from chicken at all, but rather from the legs of the crapaud, a large frog found in the island's mountainous areas. Available seasonally (late fall to early spring), it is often served in a spicy creole sauce. Fresh fish and other seafood are served in many ways. Stuffed crab backs, also available only from late fall to early spring, are a spicy and delicious option.

Feeling adventureous? Try "goat water," an odd-sounding but superb light soup using vegetables and goat meat. For something simpler, try a rich pumpkin soup or the tasty *callaloo*, a creamy soup made from the leaves of the dasheen plant. *Rotis*—curried meat, chicken or fish rolled in flatbread—are excellent, as are *titiri ackras*, fried cakes made from a tiny fresh-water fish.

Shopping

Local arts and crafts are on the forefront for the discerning buyer. In the Carib Territory, look for the centuries-old art of L'arouma reed weavings. The reeds are buried in mud for varying amounts of time before they are woven into distinctive items in shades of cream, tan and black. Double-woven, waterproof chests and suitcases, *catolis* (knapsacks) and baskets are authentic remnants of ancient Carib skills—some of the most authentic Caribbean souvenirs possible. Other artisans on the island have developed wonderful carving skills, producing beautifully carved planks called storyboards. Batik artists, painters and those working in other media also create dynamic reflections of island life.

Also, make it a point to check out the open-air market in Roseau on Saturday morning; it's a great place to people-watch and you'll be amazed at the variety and quality of produce available. Local food items—hot sauces, fruit juices, marmalades and Dominican coffee—are also worth seeking out.

Roseau's Saturday market is a great place to sample fresh flowers and produce.

Activities & Attractions

While Dominica is recognized and honored for its diving, it is the island's topside profile that distinguishes it as a prime Caribbean adventure-travel destination. Traveling divers generally dive in the morning and devote afternoons to hiking or another topside endeavor. Waterfall hikes and whale watching are two especially popular options, but other attractions include a range of hiking trails, historic forts, lakes, bird-watching, boat rides, visits to local villages, mountain biking and kayaking, to name just a few.

Unfortunately, exploration of Dominica's most remote corners is beyond the scope of the casual traveler. Though trails to rarely visited mountain peaks exist, they are rugged and extremely demanding—even experienced hikers and climbers have had severe accidents in these hills.

Recently, the government introduced user fees for foreign visitors entering eco-tourism sites, including national parks and other protected areas. Passes are available from car-rental agencies, tour operators, cruise ship personnel, the Forestry Office in Roseau and from a few of the sites such as Cabrits National Park and Emerald Pool.

Hike Ratings

Easy hikes are short and can be done by anyone with a minimal level of physical fitness.

Moderate hikes are longer and call for more physical stamina.

Strenuous hikes are physically demanding, take a full day and require the use of an experienced guide.

Hikes

Hiking opportunities range from quick five-minute waterfall trails—outlined in the Waterfall Hikes section—up to strenuous all-

day treks to the high peaks. The interior offers one of the finest examples of prime oceanic rainforest in the Western Hemisphere. Tall gommier, chataigner, balata and carapite trees support a thick canopy, from which hang bromeliads, orchids, mosses and ferns— all creating a home for an extraordinary community of creatures. A gossamer web of light filters through the network of leaves and vines, and the air is thick with the scent of flowers and plant life. The rich quiet of the rainforest, broken only by the enchanting calls of songbirds, insects and tree frogs, is extraordinary.

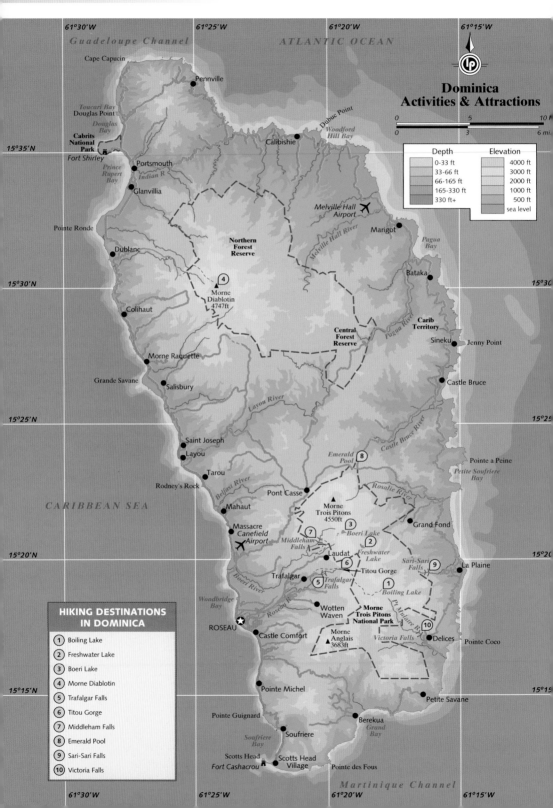

Dominica
Activities & Attractions

Depth
	0-33 ft
	33-66 ft
	66-165 ft
	165-330 ft
	330 ft+

Elevation
	4000 ft
	3000 ft
	2000 ft
	1000 ft
	500 ft
	sea level

Guadeloupe Channel
ATLANTIC OCEAN

Cape Capucin
Pennville
Toucari Bay
Douglas Point
Dubuc Point
Douglas Bay
Woodford Hill Bay
Calibishie
Cabrits National Park
Fort Shirley
Prince Rupert Bay
Portsmouth
Indian R.
Glanvillia
Melville Hall Airport
Marigot
Pagua Bay
Pointe Ronde
Melville Hall River
Dublanc
Northern Forest Reserve
Batala
Colihaut
④ Morne Diablotin 4747ft
Carib Territory
Pagua River
Sineku
Jenny Point
Morne Raquette
Central Forest Reserve
Grande Savane
Salisbury
Castle Bruce
Layou River
Saint Joseph
Layou
Castle Bruce River
Tarou
Belfast River
Rodney's Rock
Emerald Pool ⑧
Rosalie River
Pointe a Peine
Petite Soufriere Bay
Pont Casse
▲ Morne Trois Pitons 4550ft
Mahaut
Grand Fond
Boeri Lake
Massacre
Canefield Airport
⑦
③
②
Middleham Falls
Freshwater Lake
Laudat
Sari-Sari Falls
⑨
La Plaine
⑥
Titou Gorge
Trafalgar
⑤ *Trafalgar Falls*
① *Boiling Lake*
Boeri River
Woodbridge Bay
Wotten Waven
Morne Trois Pitons National Park
⑩
Delices
ROSEAU
Roseau R.
Castle Comfort
▲ Morne Anglais 3683ft
Pointe Coco
Victoria Falls
Pointe Michel
Petite Savane
Pointe Guignard
Berekua
Grand Bay
Soufriere Bay
Soufriere
Scotts Head
Fort Cashacrou
Scotts Head Village
Pointe des Fous
Martinique Channel
CARIBBEAN SEA

61°30'W   61°25'W   61°20'W   61°15'W
15°35'N
15°30'N
15°25'N
15°20'N
15°15'N

For the brave, the strong and the ambitious, there are two strenuous hikes—one to Boiling Lake and one to Morne Diablotin. A guide may not be necessary for the simplest excursions, but one is essential for more ambitious hikes. A guide will know the easiest and safest way through the hills, the potential pitfalls and dangers along the way and the history and workings of the land. A good guide will also help you spot flora and fauna, provide information about animal habits and impart local lore.

Hiking Necessities

If you plan to explore the interior, basic hiking gear is essential. Most important is a pair of good hiking boots. Make sure they have good arch and ankle support, and non-slip soles. This is a rainforest—it will most likely rain. You will need a lightweight, waterproof nylon poncho or jacket, preferably with a hood. Look for something that will fold into a small, easy-to-carry package. Also consider bringing a light pullover, as temperatures can drop in the higher altitudes.

On the longer hikes—such as Boiling Lake or Morne Diablotin—you should bring a light lunch, a high-energy snack and a bottle of water, which can be replenished at streams along the path. Most stream water is safe to drink as it comes from uninhabited slopes, but check with your guide first.

Also, it's wise to carry a simple first-aid kit. In general, keep your pack light and functional. On long hikes, every ounce makes a difference.

1 Boiling Lake   12 miles (19km)/6hrs roundtrip

Difficulty: Strenuous   **Starting Point:** 5 miles (8km) northeast of Roseau, next to Titou Gorge

The Boiling Lake hike ranks as one of Dominica's most demanding with good reason—three hours in and three hours out over some very challenging terrain. Though strenuous, the trip is an excellent way to experience the rainforest—you'll see and hear birds and other rainforest animals and get an exceptional view of the heart of the island. This trail is difficult: Do not attempt it without a local guide.

The trail itself is well maintained. The trek begins at about 1,600ft on a level stretch of rock-strewn path that alternates with wooden steps. Don't be fooled by the flat beginning—it quickly rises to a steep hill and eventually you'll be hauling yourself up the wooden steps by holding on to roots and vines. The trail

continues up and down hills until you pass the first big ridge, where you'll find a steep descent to the Breakfast River. The

Visit the world's second-largest solfatara.

river is a good place to refill your water bottle as the water is refreshingly cool, clean and safe to drink.

From the river, follow the trail to the peak of Morne Nicholls. At 3,000ft, this is the trail's maximum elevation, offering a gorgeous view of neighboring peaks, the Valley of Desolation and the steam coming off Boiling Lake. The path continues down a difficult and steep rockfall and across a volcanic plain, which is stained brown and black and teeming with smoking fumaroles. The trail leads you around a bend to the Boiling Lake, the world's second largest solfatara (water-filled volcanic crater).

Perhaps a quarter-mile across, this boiling body of water rests in the center of a volcanic crater that boasts sheer 100ft cliffs. Steam clouds—fueled by molten lava flowing just below the substrate—obscure the view of the sea and the horizon. In 1880, Boiling Lake was the source of Dominica's last major volcanic event, when a minor eruption sent clouds of ash raining on Roseau and surrounding areas.

The return trip should also take about three hours. When you get to the bottom, be sure to reward yourself with a cooling dip in Titou Gorge.

The soothing waters of Titou Gorge.

2 Freshwater Lake — 5 miles (8km)/2½hrs roundtrip

Difficulty: Moderate   **Starting Point:** 5 miles (8km) northeast of Roseau, in Laudat

Freshwater Lake rests at the end of a 2½-mile stone road that begins in the

Vibrantly colored flowers fill the rainforest.

town of Laudat. You can drive to within a 15-minute walk of the lake or walk along the road from Laudat. This is Dominica's largest lake and the source of the Roseau River. Though only 55ft deep, the lake was historically thought to be bottomless, and a persistent legend tells of a one-eyed denizen of the deep that resides in the lake. The elevated areas around the lake offer a magnificent view of the east coast and the towns of Grand Fond and Rosalie.

3 Boeri Lake
2½ miles (4km)/1½hrs roundtrip

Difficulty: Moderate   **Starting Point:** Freshwater Lake

The path to Boeri Lake begins at Freshwater Lake and is a moderate 1¼-mile walk. The path is rocky and can be slippery so be careful, especially in the rain. The lake sits at an elevation of 2,800ft and covers some four acres. As it is fed by rainfall and runoff rather than by streams, the water level varies with the seasons.

Both Freshwater and Boeri lakes sit on the lower reaches of Morne Macaque (also known locally as Morne Micotrin), a 4,000ft mountain that resulted from one of the largest volcanic eruptions in the Caribbean. This momentous eruption is thought to have occurred as long as 5 million years ago, creating a crater 1½-miles wide. You can see the worn edge of this crater from the edge of Freshwater Lake.

Daily rains offer beautiful rewards.

4 Morne Diablotin
10 miles (16km)/6–8hrs roundtrip

Difficulty: Strenuous   **Starting Point:** 4 miles (6km) south of Portsmouth, in Dublanc

The island's most challenging excursion is the hike to the peak of Morne Diablotin ("Devil's Mountain") in the Northern Forest Reserve. At 4,747ft, this is the island's highest peak and the habitat of Dominica's two endemic parrots, the jaco and the sisserou.

About 20 inches long when full grown, the sisserou is the largest of the Amazona family of parrots. It's dark purple and green. The jaco, which is smaller, is green with splashes of bright colors, including a fluff of red feathers at the throat. Neither bird is found outside of Dominica.

The hike is very difficult and takes a full day. Though this hike is shorter than the one to Boiling Lake, it is more vertical and not as well maintained near the top.

On the rare cloudless day, the peak of Morne Diablotin offers Dominica's finest possible vistas. Be sure to get started early so you can reach the peak by midday, allowing you ample opportunity for bird-watching. Even if you don't catch a glimpse of the increasingly rare native parrots, you are sure to catch sight of another of Dominica's more than 170 bird species.

The Morne Diablotin trek is rarely done—do it and you place yourself in the smallest percentage of Dominican explorers. Don't attempt it without a guide.

Waterfall Hikes

Dominica's waterfalls are among its most enticing attractions. Waterfall hikes range from a five-minute walk a grandmother could do, to a more difficult hour-long hike through the rainforest. Most of the commonly visited waterfalls are in Morne Trois Pitons National Park or near other peaks and valleys in the southern region. Organized trips are normally limited to one destination, but the determined trekker may wish to visit several in a single day.

Though many of the simpler waterfall treks can be done independently, it is wise to use a local guide for the longer ones. Fees are low and a guide will not only show you the way, but will point out plants, animals and other items of interest that you might miss on your own. Also, trail and weather conditions can be unpredictable—guides are familiar with the land and are prepared to deal with unexpected or abrupt changes.

5 Trafalgar Falls
4 miles (6km)/30min roundtrip

Difficulty: Easy **Starting Point:** 4 miles (6km) northeast of Roseau, in Trafalgar

Trafalgar Falls is actually a pair of adjacent waterfalls. The taller of the two is the Father; the shorter is the Mother. Trafalgar Falls is popular because the trail is easy and offers a grand view. From the

The Mother is the smaller of the Trafalgar Falls.

road, a 10- to 15-minute walk along a well-maintained path brings you to a viewing platform where you can see and photograph the falls. If you want to get a closer look, a path leads to the base of the falls. Paths between the falls can be a bit more demanding, so it's best to use a guide.

In 1995, the Father had an unfortunate change of face. During the middle of the night, local villagers heard a tremendous roaring sound and felt a rush of cool wind sweep through the valley. The next morning they discovered that the water-soaked cliff on the left side of the Father had collapsed, sending thousands of tons of rock hurtling down and changing its appearance forever.

Sadly, a beautiful hot spring that sat halfway up the slope was completely buried. Now, the uncertain stability of the resulting rockpile makes exploration of the left side of the Father ill-advised. The Mother remains intact, inviting you to clamber over boulders and into the pool at its base.

6 Titou Gorge
150ft (45m)/10min swim roundtrip

Difficulty: Easy   **Starting Point:** 5½ miles (9km) northeast of Roseau, in Laudat

The trip to Titou Gorge—"Little Throat" Gorge in Carib—is actually a swim to the base of a waterfall through a series of natural "rooms" formed by high walls canopied by interlaced trees. To get to the gorge, drive a half-mile beyond Laudat and look for the utility station.

The swim is short, only about five minutes, but if the water is high you won't be able to touch the bottom until you reach the end. In low-water periods, you can touch bottom along the way. Less-confident swimmers or those traveling with camera equipment may wish to use a float or BC. If you're carrying camera gear, also consider a waterproof container of some sort.

The waterfall you reach is the last of several short falls tumbling down the mountainside in a stepped series. The canopy above is spectacular, filtering the light and creating an ethereal atmosphere. In the late afternoon, the spray looks like wispy smoke. The gorge itself, with walls some 40ft tall, was formed by the grinding of a gentle stream over centuries. A hot spring that tumbles down a short wall just outside the entrance to the gorge offers a soothing, warm soak after the cool waters of the falls.

7 Middleham Falls
3½ miles (6km)/3hrs roundtrip

Difficulty: Moderate   **Starting Point:** 5 miles (8km) northeast of Roseau, in Laudat

The trek to Middleham Falls leads into the heart of the rainforest. The falls are striking—a narrow stream drops about 200ft from a keyhole notch in the lip of the cliff. Take time to strip down and brace yourself for a chilly dip. A shallow cave to the left of the falls makes a great place to sit and watch the action before diving into the water.

Though there are two trails to Middleham, the more popular trail begins off the Roseau–Laudat road high above the Roseau Valley. Once you get to Laudat, you'll need to continue down a new, well-marked dirt road leading to the Welcome Center. Here, the trailhead is less than two miles from the falls. You start at around 1,600ft, climb to a ridge at 2,200ft and then descend to the falls themselves, which are at an elevation slightly lower than where you started. The hike nor-

mally takes about three hours roundtrip. Though relatively long and hilly, the trail is not especially difficult. The hike can be done on your own, but the trail is not as well maintained as it once was. Using a guide will help ensure that you don't get hurt or lost.

8 Emerald Pool ¼ mile (.5km)/10 min roundtrip

Difficulty: Easy   **Starting Point:** 8 miles (13km) northeast of Roseau, off the Castle Bruce road

Serene Emerald Pool is just off a main road.

Tucked just five minutes off the interior Canefield–Castle Bruce road, Emerald Pool is Dominica's most accessible waterfall and draws many casual visitors. The well-marked entrance lies a half-mile beyond the junction with the road to Rosalie. From there, a walkway made of natural wooden steps leads to a peaceful 40ft waterfall. Cross a small bridge and you will find yourself in the midst of a peaceful natural rock garden. The water falls from the middle of a short vine-draped wall—the water seems to spring from the face of the rock itself. The pool at the bottom is good for wading or swimming. Emerald Pool sits on the edge of the rainforest, so it is an easy way to experience the interior with a minimum of effort.

9 Sari-Sari Falls 2 miles (3km)/2hrs roundtrip

Difficulty: Moderate   **Starting Point:** La Plaine (southeast coast)

Sari-Sari Falls are approached from the east coast road. After parking, you hike through a banana field, descending down a steep incline to the bed of the Sari-Sari River. From there, you must travel along the riverbed, climbing over boulders and crossing back and forth over the river. The exact path you travel depends on the flow of the river. The hike is short—only about a mile each way—and shouldn't take more than an hour.

Sari-Sari is a beautiful waterfall, but most of its appeal is its location on the remote Atlantic side of the island. The trip there and back gives you a chance to see the beauty of Dominica's other, less-visited coast.

The path to Sari-Sari Falls is a rocky riverbed.

10 Victoria Falls
2½ miles (4km)/1½hrs roundtrip

Difficulty: Moderate   **Starting Point:** Delices (southeast coast)

Also approached from the east coast of Dominica, a trip to Victoria Falls is best combined with a visit to Sari-Sari Falls. The trailheads are close together and each is relatively short, so you can easily see both in an afternoon's outing.

Victoria Falls is fed by the White River. The river is named for the milky color of the water from its main source, Boiling Lake. The mineral content of the water also lends the falls the same ruddy white color as the river, while the cliff face and the boulders at the base of the falls show a rich rust color from mineral deposits. By the way, don't drink the water—it tastes bad and can't be good for you.

To get to the trailhead, drive down a dirt road through the village of Delices and stop near the river. To get to the falls, make your way to the riverbed, crossing

it several times. The last 15 minutes involves walking up the river gorge and climbing over boulders. The hike should take less than 45 minutes each way.

The desolate east coast receives few visitors.

Excursions

Boat rides along **Indian River** offer a relaxed float up a placid stream. This is the ultimate effortless excursion—all the work is done by the boatman. At the mouth of the river, less than a mile south of Portsmouth, you'll find a fleet of colorfully painted boats. Just go there, find a boatman and begin negotiating prices. Prices don't vary much so you should look for a boatman with whom you

feel comfortable. Though some of the boats have motors, a boat with oars is preferable. You can lie back and relax as you travel up a beautiful stream under a latticework of luxuriant vegetation, listening to the chatter of wildlife rather than the drone of a motor. The boats stop below a small rapids about a mile upstream. Nearby, local vendors have stands where you can buy rum punch and Kabuli beer (the local Dominican brew).

A boat without a motor is the best way to enjoy the wildlife along the Indian River.

Cabrits National Park, north of Portsmouth, is a fine place for the entire family to explore. This distinctive peninsula is the northern border of Prince Rupert Bay and the shoreline here is home to several good snorkeling and diving sites. The headland of this peninsula is formed by a pair of extinct volcanoes called the Cabrits. The steep slopes of the peninsula, surrounded on three sides by the transparent turquoise and azure sea, are thickly coated with ferns and trees.

The historic focus of the park is **Fort Shirley**, on the southern side of the peninsula. Built by both the French and British, the complex comprises more than fifty structures on the 260-acre peninsula. During the 18th and 19th centuries, the fort provided protection to naval and civilian vessels anchored in the bay. Today, the fort is in an ongoing state of restoration to its former glory.

Dominica's other important military structure is **Fort Cashacrou**, a small platform at the peak of Scotts Head, the extreme southern point of the island. This tiny peninsula was called Cashacrou by the Carib Indians. If you have a 4-wheel-drive vehicle, you can drive the road to Fort Cashacrou. Otherwise, park near the bottom and walk up the hill—it only takes a few minutes. At the peak you will find a cannon, which was used to warn of French boats approaching from across the Martinique Channel. Nearby, a lone cross is dedicated to fishermen returning home from the sea. The headland also offers excellent views of Soufriere Bay and Martinique.

Fort Cashacrou's cannon once warned of French ships approaching from Martinique.

Make time for a visit to the **Botanical Gardens** in eastern Roseau. The 40-acre gardens feature an aviary and breeding facility for Dominica's native parrots, the jaco and the sisserou. There are also many distinctly labeled native trees and flowering tropical shrubs. If you have questions, simply stop by the Forestry Office for pamphlets and conversation. The gardens also house a monument of sorts to the forces of 1979's Hurricane David—a school bus crushed under the weight of an enormous native tree.

Native tropical plants, like this flowering ixora, are maintained at the Botanical Gardens.

There are numerous other places to visit around the island, far too many to detail. Take time to visit the villages around the coast. Traverse the **Indiana Jones Bridge**, a suspension bridge across the Layou River. Relax in hot springs at Wotten Waven, Sulphur Springs, Layou or any of a dozen other lesser-known spots. Adventure is the key word in Dominica—ask people what's interesting and you'll surely find secret spots!

Kayaking

Several dive operators rent ocean kayaks suitable for carrying a single diver with dive or snorkel gear. For the independent diver, a kayak is a nice alternative to a boat ride or long swim and serves as a platform upon which to rest between dives. For snorkelers and nondivers, kayaking is a great way to skirt the shoreline, viewing the waters below and choosing your own explorations. Ocean kayaks are available at **Nature Island Dive** in Soufriere and at **Cabrits Dive Centre** in Portsmouth. From Soufriere, the best kayaking is in the bay and around Scotts Head. From Portsmouth you will want to paddle around the Cabrits and possibly along the coast in Douglas Bay and Toucari Bay. In either location you will pass over some of the island's best shallow reefs, so be sure to bring snorkel gear.

Kayakers in Soufriere Bay beach their crafts at the base of Scotts Head.

Mountain Biking

For the reasonably fit traveler, biking is a great way to explore the island. **Nature Island Dive** in Soufriere rents mountain bikes. The folks at the shop have maps of some of the best routes in the southern region. The trails take you through the hills above Soufriere, leading to sulphur springs, old ruins or along scenic paths. For the more experienced cyclist, the possibilities are extensive, especially if you have car access to other parts of the island. Be extremely cautious when riding on the roads—they are narrow and people drive fast. The price of the rental includes a helmet—wear it both on the streets and off-road!

Whale Watching

Dominica is considered one the finest destinations in the Caribbean for cetacean—that is, whale, dolphin and porpoise—encounters. Recently, a group of researchers spent several months documenting whales and dolphins around Dominica and discovered an astounding number of species. No one is sure exactly why these creatures are attracted to the area, but the deep waters and an abundant food supply certainly play a part.

Whale-watching excursions have become daily endeavors off the coast of Dominica. The best vessels offer dedicated whale- and/or dolphin-watching trips complete with experienced sighters and sensitive hydrophones for locating the animals and listening to their clicks and calls. **Dive Dominica** and **Anchorage Dive Centre** are two of the most dependable operations—both use directional and omni-directional hydrophones and have years of experience. Boats usually leave in the afternoon for the three- to four-hour trip. If you are prone to seasickness, you may want to consider suitable medication. It is important to note that cetacean encounters are common but unpredictable. As they say, "you pays your money and you takes your chances."

Sperm whales feed chiefly on squid, octopus and cuttlefish. In search of prey, they can dive to 3,000ft (900m) and stay under for as much as 45 minutes.

Festive Carnival

Colorful, elaborate costume parades are part of the Carnival tradition.

Held during the traditional Mardi Gras period in the two weeks prior to Lent, Carnival is Dominica's biggest and most colorful annual event. The spring holiday's myriad activities include calypso competitions, costume parades and a Carnival Queen contest.

The most intense Carnival celebrations occur during J'ouvert, the Monday and Tuesday—that is, Fat Tuesday or *Mardi Gras* in French—before Ash Wednesday. Food, drink, dancing, sweat, smiles and laughter are rampant.

Among the most captivating highlights of Dominica's festival are spontaneous local dances called jump-ups. During the jump-ups, writhing seas of people dance and shout, following a slow-moving truck piled high with speakers blasting chest-quaking music.

Be forewarned: This is the time when crime is most rampant on the island. The crowded and drunken festivities are a big draw to pickpockets and other thieves, largely from off-island. Use a money belt rather than a wallet. Separate your money into several pockets, preferably ones that can be closed with buttons or zippers. Remove jewelry, especially necklaces, bracelets and valuable watches that can be snatched easily.

Diving Health & Safety

General Health

Your general state of health, diving skill level and specific equipment needs are the three most important factors of any dive trip. If you honestly assess these before you leave, and even before selecting your dive destination, you'll be well on your way to a safe and successful dive trip.

First, if you're not in shape, start exercising. Second, if you haven't dived for a while (six months is too long) and your skills are rusty, do a local dive with an experienced buddy or take a scuba review course. Finally, inspect your dive gear. Feeling good physically, diving with experience and using reliable equipment will not only increase your safety, but will also enhance your enjoyment underwater.

Though Dominica is relatively disease-free, with standard traveler's diarrhea topping the list of health-related concerns, it's wise to check for any recent developments. Contact the U.S. Centers for Disease Control for updates by fax or via the web. Call (toll-free from the U.S.) ☎ 888-CDC-FAXX and request Document 000005. The website is www.cdc.gov.

Pre-Trip Preparation

At least a month before you leave, inspect your dive gear. Remember, your regulator should be serviced annually, whether you've used it or not. If you use a dive computer and can replace the battery yourself, change it before the trip or buy a spare one to take along. Otherwise, send the computer to the manufacturer for a battery replacement.

If possible, find out if the dive center rents or services the type of gear you own. If not, you might want to take spare parts or even spare gear. A spare mask is always a good idea.

Purchase any additional equipment you might need, such as a dive light and tank marker light for night diving, a line reel for wreck diving, etc. Make sure you have at least a whistle attached to your BC. Even better, add a marker tube (also known as a safety sausage or come-to-me).

About a week before taking off, do a final check of your gear, grease o-rings, check batteries and assemble a save-a-dive kit (and possibly a first-aid kit). Don't forget to fill prescriptions and pack medications such as decongestants, ear drops, antihistamines and seasick tablets.

Pre-trip planning is always wise, but for a scuba trip, it's critical. Be careful not to "get in over your head," so to speak. Standards vary among countries and among dive operations. If you have little diving experience, it would be wise to select a relatively popular area that sees a lot of new divers, has modern medical facilities and provides reliable rental gear. On the other hand, if you're in good shape, dive a lot and have your own gear, you might choose a more remote area that requires greater self-reliance.

Tips for Evaluating a Dive Boat

A well-outfitted dive boat can communicate with services onshore and carries oxygen, a recall device and a first-aid kit. The crew will explain procedures for dealing with an emergency when divers are in the water and will give a thorough pre-dive briefing, which includes how divers should enter the water and get back on board. Larger boats will have a shaded area and supply fresh drinking water.

In a strong current, the crew can throw out a drift line from the stern and use a special descent line. For deep dives, they'll hang a safety tank at 15ft (4.5m). On night dives, they'll have powerful lights, including a strobe light.

When carrying groups, one of the most important tasks the crew will perform is getting everyone's name on the dive roster. This is something you should always verify, so that the crew can immediately initiate a search if you don't appear back on board.

Medical & Recompression Facilities

There is no recompression chamber on Dominica. There are chambers on Martinique and St. Lucia, but they are not considered dependable and may not be in working order. In a dive emergency, divers would most likely be evacuated to the U.S. (and later be billed several thousand dollars for the service). All traveling divers should purchase insurance that covers emergency medical evacuation.

Dominica's local health clinics, listed below, can help with minor medical emergencies, but may not be appropriate for more serious problems.

Grand Bay Health Centre
Grand Bay (south coast)
☎ 446-3706

Portsmouth Hospital
Portsmouth
☎ 445-5237

Marigot Hospital
Marigot (east coast)
☎ 445-7091

Princess Margaret Hospital
Roseau
☎ 448-2231

Deep Diving

There are many opportunities to dive deep in Dominica. At many sites, the best features are found beyond 130ft (40m), which is considered the maximum depth limit of sport diving. Before venturing beyond these limits, you must be specially trained in deep diving and/or technical diving.

Classes will teach you to recognize symptoms of nitrogen narcosis and to perform proper decompression procedures for deep or repetitive deep dives. Emergency facilities in Dominica are limited. Know your limits and don't push your luck when it comes to depth.

DAN

Divers Alert Network (DAN) is an international membership association of individuals and organizations sharing a common interest in diving and safety. It operates a 24-hour diving emergency hotline, ☎ 919-684-8111 or ☎ 919-684-4326. The latter accepts collect calls in a dive emergency. DAN does not directly provide medical care; however, it does provide advice on early treatment, evacuation and hyperbaric treatment of diving-related injuries. Divers should contact DAN for assistance as soon as a diving emergency is suspected. DAN membership is reasonably priced and includes DAN TravelAssist, a membership benefit that covers medical air evacuation from anywhere in the world for any illness or injury. For a small additional fee, divers can get secondary insurance coverage for decompression illness. For membership questions, ☎ 800-446-2671 in the U.S. or ☎ 919-684-2948 elsewhere.

By day, glassy sweepers prefer darker areas such as the cavern at Pointe Guignard.

Diving in Dominica

Many diving islands are arid and flat, with very little silt-bearing freshwater runoff to ruin visibility. In Dominica, however, copious rainfall and a rugged terrain mean plenty of runoff, yet visibility remains excellent. Because the waters surrounding Dominica are remarkably deep, the silt quickly falls away, providing a steady nutrient-rich food source for the area's underwater inhabitants. The result is incredibly vital invertebrate growth. Filter-feeders grow like crazy. Crinoids perch on sponges with arms extended, drawing the maximum benefit from this rich water. Sponge, hard coral and gorgonian growth is superb and vibrantly healthy.

Even the reefs are unique. Most coral reefs are porous biological structures and a large portion of the inhabitants live in the reef's cracks and crevices. Dominica's reefs are solid geological masses—boulders and sheer granite faces to which sessile creatures adhere. Since all creatures must reside on the exterior of the reef, the visible population is larger than normal and interactions between creatures are sometimes atypical.

Diving in Dominica has been well established for years. Boats range from small six-person skiffs to larger catamarans that handle groups of 16 or more. Staff is well

Home to many popular dive sites, Soufriere Bay is made up of a submerged volcanic crater.

trained and is generally split between native Dominicans and expatriates from the U.S., Canada and Europe.

For divers, special considerations include high currents in the more extreme areas and the general potential for reaching extreme depths. All divers must take particular care to monitor depth when over walls or on the sides of pinnacles; computers are recommended. Shore diving is not prevalent, in part because local law holds that divers must always be accompanied by a government-registered, licensed divemaster whether diving from boat or shore. Additionally, shore access is often rocky and difficult, especially with equipment.

This book divides dive sites into three regional sections: Southern, Mid-Island and Northern Dive Sites. While the southern sites—which surround a submerged volcanic crater in Soufriere Bay—are popular, the variety provided by the mid-island and northern sites is not to be missed. For each site, the underwater terrain and common marine life are described in detail, along with information on location, depth range, expertise rating and access.

Certification

Most dive operations are PADI 5-Star resorts and all offer instruction up to divemaster. NAUI certification is also available. If you have recently completed your

Snorkeling in Dominica

A snorkel, mask and fins are all you need to begin exploring Dominica's underwater wonders. Virtually every dive operator offers dedicated snorkeling trips and some put snorkelers and divers on the same boat when the site is appropriate for both.

If possible, bring your own snorkeling gear. If you do need gear, any dive operator has masks, fins, snorkels and life vests for rent. Be sure that the staff helps you find equipment that fits properly.

Because of Dominica's rough terrain, shore access is difficult or impossible in many areas. Also, boat traffic can be a problem in some areas, so snorkeling from a recognized dive vessel is often the best option. Another idea is to snorkel from a kayak, which can be rented from several dive shops. This puts shallow sites around Scotts Head in the south or the Cabrits Peninsula in the north within reach of the independent snorkeler.

Among the best sites for snorkeling are Soufriere Pinnacles, Champagne and Pointe Guignard to the south; Rodney's Rock in the mid-island section; and the shoreline around the Cabrits Peninsula, Toucari Bay Point and Douglas Bay Point to the north.

classroom and pool work at home, you may want to consider doing your open-water dives in Dominica. If you have never had the opportunity to dive, there are plenty of shallow sites ideal for a resort course. A resort course consists of a few hours of instruction and training with equipment followed by an instructor-accompanied dive to 40ft (12m). Though not a certification, a resort course allows you to experience a dive and get a first glimpse into the underwater world.

Dive Site Icons

The symbols at the beginning of the dive site descriptions provide a quick summary of some of the following characteristics present at the site:

 Good snorkeling or free-diving site.

 Remains or partial remains of a wreck can be seen at this site.

 Sheer wall or drop-off.

 Deep dive. Features of this dive occur in water deeper than 90ft (27m).

 Strong currents may be encountered at this site.

 Strong surge (the horizontal movement of water caused by waves) may be encountered at this site.

 Drift dive. Because of strong currents and/or difficulty in anchoring, a drift dive is recommended at this site.

 Beach/shore dive. This site can be accessed from shore.

 Poor visibility. The site often has visibility of less than 25ft (8m).

 Caves are a prominent feature of this site. Only experienced cave divers should explore inner cave areas.

 Marine preserve. Special regulations apply in this area.

Pisces Rating System for Dives & Divers

The dive sites in this book are rated according to the following diver skill-level rating system. These are not absolute ratings but apply to divers at a particular time, diving at a particular place. For instance, someone unfamiliar with prevailing conditions might be a novice diver at one dive area, but an intermediate diver at another, more familiar location.

Novice: A novice diver generally fits the following profile:
◆ basic scuba certification from an internationally recognized certifying agency
◆ dives infrequently (less than one trip a year)
◆ logged fewer than 25 total dives
◆ dives no deeper than 60ft (18m)
◆ little or no experience diving in similar waters and conditions
* *A novice diver should be accompanied by an instructor, divemaster or advanced diver on all dives*

Intermediate: An intermediate diver generally fits the following profile:
◆ may have participated in some form of continuing diver education
◆ logged between 25 and 100 dives
◆ dives no deeper than 130ft (40m)
◆ has been diving within the last six months in similar waters and conditions

Advanced: An advanced diver generally fits the following profile:
◆ advanced certification
◆ has been diving for more than two years and logged more than 100 dives
◆ has been diving within the last six months in similar waters and conditions

Regardless of skill level, you should be in good physical condition and know your limitations. If you are uncertain as to your own level of expertise, ask the advice of a local dive instructor. He or she is best qualified to assess your abilities based on the prevailing dive conditions at any given site. Ultimately you must decide if you are capable of making a particular dive, depending on your level of training, recent experience and physical condition, as well as water conditions at the site. Remember that water conditions can change at any time, even during a dive.

Huge clusters of sponges topped with crinoids are a hallmark of Dominican diving.

Southern Dive Sites

The southern region is home to Dominica's most popular dive sites—and with good reason. The highlight of the south, the Soufriere Bay, is perhaps the most distinctive area of Dominican diving. The entire bay is formed and defined by the submerged crater of an underwater volcano. The east edge of the crater is the shoreline, while the south edge is the Scotts Head promontory. The crater's north edge is submerged, but the underwater pinnacles nearly reach the surface. The west edge of the crater is too deep for recreational diving.

The Soufriere dive sites reflect the volcanic action that created them—deep walls, pinnacles, massive boulders, chasms and gullies offer some of the island's most dramatic diving. Dive sites are also found off the southern coast in the Martinique Channel. These are more challenging due to high current conditions, but offer highly variegated wall formations and a greater chance to see deep-water pelagics. North of Soufriere Bay are several fascinating shallow sites, most based just off the shoreline.

The hills of the southwest coast continue their sharp descent under the water.

Southern Dive Sites

	Good Snorkeling	Novice	Intermediate	Advanced
1 Des Fous				●
2 Lost Horizons			●	
3 Suburbs			●	
4 Village				●
5 Condo			●	
6 Mountain Top				●
7 Swiss Cheese	●		●	
8 Scotts Head Pinnacle	●		●	
9 Cashacrou (Crater's Edge)			●	
10 Scotts Head Point	●		●	
11 Scotts Head Drop-Off	●		●	
12 Soufriere Pinnacles	●		●	
13 La Sorciere			●	
14 L'Abym			●	
15 Coral Gardens South	●	●		
16 Dangleben's Pinnacles			●	
17 Dangleben's North	●		●	
18 Pointe Guignard	●	●		
19 Champagne	●	●		

1 Des Fous

Directly off Pointe des Fous, this site represents some of the wildest diving Dominica has to offer. Des Fous sits farther east than any other recognized Dominican dive site and is subject to rough seas and strong, potentially dangerous currents. It is suitable for only the very experienced diver.

Just a few operators visit this site and only when conditions are favorable, usually just a few times a year. Divers who do get the opportunity are rewarded with a striking reef face and an abundance of life, including both schooling fish and pelagics.

The dive plan varies according to the direction of the current. Divers normally descend on the east side, where a vertical wall begins in just 25ft. From there, you move west with the current along

Location: South of Pointe des Fous

Depth Range: 25–130ft (8–40m)

Access: Boat

Expertise Rating: Advanced

the face of the wall, gradually descending to a coral shelf on the west side of the point.

The wall is thickly overgrown, decorated with large sea fans, gorgonians, sponges and black coral. Overhangs provide shelter for schooling snapper and chub. On the point there is a small cave at 130ft, but penetration of this cubbyhole is not recommended. Check under the coral ledges for resting nurse sharks.

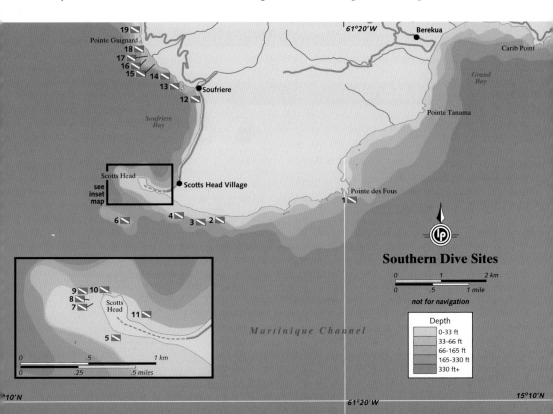

Southern Dive Sites

Depth	
	0-33 ft
	33-66 ft
	66-165 ft
	165-330 ft
	330 ft+

not for navigation

Once you reach the shallow coral shelf, you can pass through a wave-etched arch or check out shallow hollows along the shoreline. Be cautious, as there can often be a strong surge in the shallows. In general, be sure to keep an eye on the deep blue: The swift currents make it a favored area for whitetip and mako sharks, large tuna, jacks and barracuda.

Complex structures of black coral, sea fans and sponges adorn a wall.

2 Lost Horizons

This narrow gully—a split in the reef—leads out into the blue water of the Martinique Channel. The gully is draped with thick clusters of deep-sea gorgonians interspersed with stands of various types of sponges. Move to the right after you come out of this reef valley and you will find a steep but not quite vertical wall.

Huge barrel sponges, some easily 6ft tall and 3ft across, are a prominent feature of this enticing site. Large schools of fish meander in from the deep blue to visit the reef. The upper shelf, which is dominated by masses of sea fans, eventually leads to a short overhanging wall rich

Location: Southeast of Scotts Head Village

Depth Range: 25–100ft (8–30m)

Access: Boat

Expertise Rating: Intermediate

with invertebrate growth. Eventually, the wall drops to depths beyond sport-diving limits. As with all sites in the Martinique Channel, strong currents are always a possibility.

3 Suburbs

Diving at Suburbs can be a thrilling experience, though there is potential for strong currents and heavy swells on the surface. The draw for divers is the wealth of life, particularly filter feeders such as sponges, gorgonians and crinoids. The sponges here have grown to monstrous sizes, as have the curtains of gorgonians.

Fish life—generally large schools of snapper, black durgon, southern sennet and marauding barracuda—lurk in gaps in the reef. Turtles have been seen here, as have other larger life forms like the spotted eagle ray.

The mooring sits at 47ft and is attached to the northern edge of the first shelf. A short wall draped with black coral drops to a second narrow shelf at 55ft. Below the second shelf, the wall plunges vertically into the depths. The site's main focus is a large rocky outcropping extending from the western edge of

Location: Southeast of Scotts Head Village

Depth Range: 25–130ft (8–40m)

Access: Boat

Expertise Rating: Intermediate

the shelf. Gorgonian-draped overhangs on the outcropping and on the wall shelter abundant of marine life.

A crinoid combs the water for plankton.

Schooling gray snapper prefer gaps in the reef.

Dominica's Whales & Dolphins

Dominica has recorded sightings of over a dozen species of cetaceans (whales, dolphins and porpoises). Following are descriptions of four of the most commonly seen species.

Pantropical Spotted Dolphin
Stenalla attenuata Spotted dolphins, which can grow up to 7ft long, are most easily distinguished by the light-colored spots covering their bodies. The juvenile is unspotted, gradually developing markings with age. Spotted dolphins travel in pods of 50 or more, often mixing with bottlenose dolphins. This species is similar to the Atlantic spotted dolphin, also found in Dominica, which has spots at birth that gradually fade with age.

Sperm Whale
Physeter catodon The male sperm whale can grow up to 60ft long, though 30–40ft adult males are more common. It is distinguished by a huge box-like head with a single blowhole on the left side of the forehead. They dive to 3,000ft and are thought to feed on giant squid, an impressive foe possibly 20–30ft in length. In fact, sperm whales with sucker impressions the size of a dinner plate have been seen! Sperm whales can dive for

45 minutes and more. Following a dive, they will rest on the surface for up to 15 minutes.

Short-Finned Pilot Whale
Globicephala macrorhyndchus Males can grow up to 18ft long and females may reach 13ft. The short-finned pilot whale is distinguished by its thick, rounded head and curved dorsal fin with a rounded tip. These whales tend to travel in pods of 15 to 50.

Spinner Dolphin
Stenella longirotris Spinner dolphins can reach lengths of 5–7ft with males slightly larger than females. Slender with a long, narrow head, the spinner has a triangular dorsal fin and a black-tipped snout and lips. This dolphin is common and is frequently seen in pods of 200 or more. The spinner is named for its distinctive habit of leaping out of the water and spinning horizontally.

TIM ROCK

4 Village

Village is not for the faint-hearted or out-of-shape diver. Like Suburbs, Village may be subject to strong currents and this site in particular seems to have a stronger surge than many others. A shelf at about 35ft leads down to a nearly vertical wall. As it gets deeper, the slope of the wall becomes more gradual as it drops into the Martinique Channel.

Three granite outcroppings—the first at 45ft, the second at 65ft and the final at around 85ft—are dominant topographic features. On the eastern sides of these outcroppings, you'll find large sea fans interspersed with small forests of deep-sea gorgonians. Hard corals and large sponge clusters also stand out.

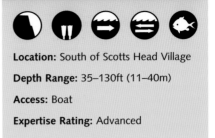

Location: South of Scotts Head Village

Depth Range: 35–130ft (11–40m)

Access: Boat

Expertise Rating: Advanced

Look for schools of stalking barracuda hanging just on the edge of visibility, occasionally swooping in to get a closer look at divers. Also, keep an eye on the open water, as you never know what might swim past. Even if nothing large materializes, the reef itself will provide enough action to keep you riveted.

5 Condo

Condo is a highly unusual site. The surrounding sand and rock bottom supports a community of large barrel sponges along with a healthy population of fish and smaller invertebrates.

Smack-dab in the middle of this is a massive rock with a circular, flat-topped shape. It is generally assumed that the stone was once part of the crater cap of the Soufriere volcano. When the volcano blew its top, the crater cap fragmented and this piece was thrown over Scotts Head and into the sea, settling in the sand where it now rests.

Sitting in about 55ft, the stone tops off at just 18ft. Currents can kick up a bit but

Location: South of Scotts Head Point

Depth Range: 18–55ft (6–17m)

Access: Boat

Expertise Rating: Intermediate

the stone offers a lee side no matter what direction the current's running. Cracks, crevices and narrow fissures run through the stone, creating perfect hideaways for smaller creatures and schooling fish. Look for the rare red-banded lobster. Schooling blackbar soldierfish are common residents. The rock's exterior is adorned with thick growths of both soft and hard corals.

Condo is a short dive; it takes only about 20 minutes or so to explore the circumference. Try circling the stone at depth slowly and then again in the shallower depths, checking out the top on your final pass. Watch for the large southern stingray frequently sighted here.

Sea fans and sea spray drape Condo's exterior.

Blackbar soldierfish take shelter in a crevice.

6 Mountain Top

About a mile southwest of Scotts Head Point, this site is the top of a seamount rising from the depths of the Martinique Channel. Mountain Top is a relatively deep dive and, because of its unprotected location, is subject to strong currents. When conditions are right, however, it is a spectacular dive.

Location: About 1 mile (1.5km) south of Scotts Head Point

Depth Range: 55–130ft (17–40m)

Access: Boat

Expertise Rating: Advanced

The mooring is in 67ft and from there, the wall drops off on all sides into the deep blue. The seamount, with its overhangs, mini-walls and crevices, supports large and lush deep-sea gorgonians and black coral trees, as well as some very healthy hard corals.

The open-water location attracts large schools of snapper and horse-eye jacks, larger barracuda and an occasional shark, turtle, southern stingray or manta ray. Check under ledges and in crevices for lobster. This is a truly monster site with huge potential. If you are diving the south and have the requisite expertise, put it on the top of your request list!

Schools of horse-eye jacks roam Mountain Top's waters.

7 Swiss Cheese

Part of the Scotts Head Pinnacle complex, Swiss Cheese is a large granite rock named for the honeycomb-like structure of the reef. Riddled with nooks and crannies, Swiss Cheese provides shelter for a fascinating variety of schooling fish and invertebrate life, including sponges and deep-sea gorgonians. Blackbar soldierfish mix with large schools of grunts, Bermuda chub, barracuda, and the occasional southern stingray.

Location: West of Scotts Head Point

Depth Range: 15–50ft (5–15m)

Access: Boat

Expertise Rating: Intermediate

Swiss Cheese can be done as a separate dive, but is often the entry and exit point

Schooling grunts are wary of approaching divers.

of a Scotts Head Pinnacle dive. A swim-through at the bottom of the rock at 30ft emerges at 18ft, creating an ideal spot for a safety stop at the end of your dive. There is plenty of life to observe in shallow water near the peak of the rock while you get rid of a little nitrogen.

8 Scotts Head Pinnacle

Scotts Head Pinnacle is just to the west of Swiss Cheese and is part of the same complex. The two dives are frequently combined: Divers begin at Swiss Cheese, pass through a couple of swim-throughs, circle some small pinnacles and approach a gorgeous archway in the middle of the main pinnacle.

Location: West of Scotts Head Point

Depth Range: 5–80ft (2–24m)

Access: Boat or shore

Expertise Rating: Novice

This arch, located at about 40ft, is formed by two massive granite boulders leaning against one another. The growth inside tends to change with time. One year a strong tropical storm or hurricane might create a surge that will scrub the walls clean, but a year later it might once again sport a coating of telesto corals, other soft corals and encrusting

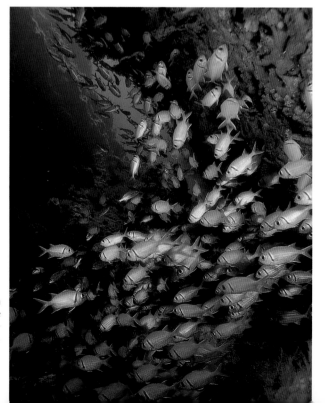

Blackbar soldierfish orient themselves to the arch, sometimes swimming upside down.

sponges. Regular inhabitants of this 50ft-long archway often include large schools of blackbar soldierfish and a mixed school of grunts.

To end the dive, pass through the arch, circle to the left, go around the pinnacle and return to the top of Swiss Cheese for a safety stop.

9 Cashacrou (Crater's Edge)

Cashacrou sits on the westernmost diveable edge of the Soufriere crater, northwest of Scotts Head. Here, nutrient-rich waters well up from the Martinique Channel, creating strong surge conditions as they wash over the shallow reef shelf. These waters provide an excellent feeding ground for fish and filter-feeding invertebrates.

The short wall skirting Cashacrou is cloaked with deep-sea gorgonians and sponges, and a crack at 90ft is home to a large school of black margate. The nutrient cycling fosters an abundant population of smaller critters, which in

Location: West of Scotts Head Point

Depth Range: 30–90ft (9–27m)

Access: Boat

Expertise Rating: Intermediate

turn attract schools of larger fish. The schooling fish, of course, attract larger predators from the deep, making this a great spot to witness the food chain in action. As they say, "de big fish eat de little fish" and so it goes on down the line.

Considered living fossils, crinoids (also called feather stars) have changed little since ancient times.

10 Scotts Head Point

This site is just off the headland point and has all the glories you come to expect from the southern region. Scotts Head Point can be approached from two different directions. The north side is a vertical wall that starts in shallow water and drops into the heart of the crater. Despite the vertical wall, it is excellent for snorkeling because of the shallow

Location: North of Scotts Head Point

Depth Range: 7–90ft (2–27m)

Access: Boat or shore

Expertise Rating: Intermediate

reef areas at the top. Currents here are usually minimal.

A second approach is to dive the west edge, which has a vastly different topography than the north side. This side represents its violent volcanic origins with a field of massive granite outcroppings scattered down the reef slope, creating canyons and gullies. Here, currents can be a bit more severe.

Both sides of the point boast an excellent marine population. One of the rare inhabitants is the red-banded lobster, a small lobster sighted more frequently here than anywhere else on the island.

A diver admires a barrel sponge adorned with crinoids.

At night, the rare red-banded lobster forgages for food near crevice openings.

11 Scotts Head Drop-Off

Scotts Head Drop-Off is a flexible site with easy shore access for snorkeling. Shore entry is from Trousable, a small beach at the base of the Scotts Head peninsula. From there, you pass over a very shallow shelf before proceeding into deep water. This is the southern lip of the Soufriere crater and exhibits all the marine life and topographic characteristics associated with this area. The reef's many overhangs shelter schooling reef fish and smaller barracuda, Bermuda chub and boga. The reef extends out from shore at an average depth of 30ft before dropping to 90ft and then sloping off into the depths of Soufriere Bay.

This area is heavily used by local fishermen, so you will see fish traps and a lot of debris on the bottom. Also, passing yachts have done significant anchor

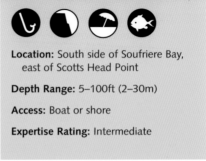

Location: South side of Soufriere Bay, east of Scotts Head Point

Depth Range: 5–100ft (2–30m)

Access: Boat or shore

Expertise Rating: Intermediate

damage. Many visiting divers are understandably alarmed and offended by the degradation of the site.

It is important to understand that education about environmental concerns is a gradual but ongoing process. Awareness is growing and, with proper management, the site is expected to recover. Fortunately, even in its present condition, this site offers enough marine life to keep a diver coming back again and again.

A pair of schoolmasters eyes a diver warily.

12 Soufriere Pinnacles

The Soufriere Pinnacles offer classic southern Dominica diving. Here, three separate pinnacles rise from a shelf resting in 35ft, with the tallest coming to within just a few feet of the surface. Situated in front of Soufriere's picturesque Catholic church, the site can be accessed either by boat or from the shore.

The 300ft swim from shore passes over bubbling submerged hot springs and gas vents with plenty of tiny fish darting about. Easy access, shallow depths and fascinating structures make this site ideal for snorkelers.

Location: West of Soufriere, in front of the Catholic church

Depth Range: 5–100ft (2–30m)

Access: Boat or shore

Expertise Rating: Novice

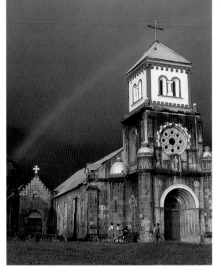

Soufriere's Catholic church overlooks the bay.

Divers can explore the west side of the pinnacles, which drop at a severe angle into the Soufriere crater. This west edge forms a portion of the L'Abym wall. Because of the site's proximity to Soufriere, one of Dominica's traditional fishing villages, coral growths at this site are less healthy than at more remote sites and large fish are unusual. That said, divers and snorkelers will discover loads of juvenile fish and a wealth of invertebrates such as golden crinoids. Seahorses and frogfish are also frequently seen here.

13 La Sorciere

This site sits directly off an isolated cliff known as La Sorciere ("The Sorceress"). Legend holds that Carib men threw unfaithful mates to their deaths from the cliff. It is believed that the unfortunate women put a curse on the site—earning the cliff a bewitching name—and that the women's souls continue to haunt the area to this very day.

Another name for the cliff is Carib's Leap and more local legend has it that Carib warriors threw themselves from

Location: North side of Soufriere Bay

Depth Range: 15–100ft (5–30m)

Access: Boat

Expertise Rating: Intermediate

the cliff rather than face enslavement by captors.

Murder, suicide and witchcraft aside, the reef below this cliff presents some hauntingly beautiful images. The mooring sits in about 15ft. Begin there and proceed west to the edge of what is a mostly vertical wall. Some areas offer narrow shelves but overhangs are uncommon and the wall quickly drops to 750ft.

The fish life here is like that found in much of the area, with brown and blue chromis in the midwater, bigeyes and blackbar soldierfish in the crevices, and lush invertebrate growth along the face of the wall. Overlapping plate corals tumble down the drop-off, interspersed with clusters of whip corals and some excellent sponge formations.

14 L'Abym

L'Abym (a creole word meaning "The Deep") sits north of La Sorciere and is one of the area's most vertical wall sites. Running roughly north to south, the wall is about two miles long and stretches to La Sorciere and beyond, extending almost to the Soufriere Pinnacles. This is the easternmost edge of the Soufriere crater and the wall plunges into the heart of the caldera, offering heart-stopping glimpses into the deep.

Extensive life forms cling to the wall. High points include sizable black coral

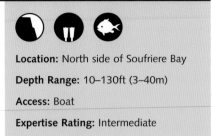

Location: North side of Soufriere Bay

Depth Range: 10–130ft (3–40m)

Access: Boat

Expertise Rating: Intermediate

trees, deep-sea gorgonians and whip corals. Due to the deeper water, there is the possibility of encountering pelagics such as tuna, jacks, rays and turtles. Smaller reef inhabitants are also prolific. Clouds of schooling midwater fish combine with the reef fish common to the area. Look on the face of the wall for seahorses wrapped around the bases and arms of gorgonians. Check for tiny shrimp nestling in the arms of anemones. Like many other Dominican sites, L'Abym is critter heaven and despite the difficulty of shooting on a wall, is excellent for macrophotography as well.

Black coral grows just a quarter-inch per year.

A shrimp cleans its host anemone.

15   Coral Gardens South

South of Dangleben's North and east of Dangleben's Pinnacles, Coral Gardens South connects with both reefs, completing the area's reef system. With the mooring in just 12ft, the site can be explored by divers and snorkelers with equal satisfaction. Here you'll find the greatest variety of hard corals—upward of 17 varieties.

Location: Southeast of Pointe Guignard

Depth Range: 12–50ft (4–15m)

Access: Boat

Expertise Rating: Novice

A large rock under the mooring leads into a patch reef that is home to tons of invertebrates. The patch reef leads to an area combining finger coral and rubble, which slopes west to a more solidly formed reef. The site's numerous overhangs provide shelter for a variety of typical reef fish and invertebrates. Sea turtles are found here periodically. As the reef slopes to the west, the water gets deeper and the sponge clusters get larger and more complex, eventually blending into the Dangleben's Pinnacles site on its northwest corner.

Worldwide, sea turtles have suffered dramatically from harvesting of eggs and meat, but they are still found in Dominican waters.

16   Dangleben's Pinnacles

One of two sites named for the Dangleben family who owned the land immediately adjacent, divers favor this site because of the varied terrain and marine life. Dangleben's Pinnacles consists of five separate pinnacles rising from the north edge of the Soufriere crater. Remarkably, each of the pinnacles supports different life forms.

Location: ½ mile (.8km) south of Pointe Guignard

Depth Range: 25–130ft (8–40m)

Access: Boat

Expertise Rating: Intermediate

The pinnacles top off as shallow as 25ft and drop to a base shelf at about 60ft. On the south side, the pinnacles plummet into the heart of the crater, reaching depths beyond sport-diving limits.

While there are similarities in fish life—look for schools of horse-eye jacks, silversides and blackbar soldierfish—it is the larger sessile invertebrates that distinguish one pinnacle from another. On one wall you will find a forest of black coral trees, on the next, massive clusters of yellow tube sponges dominate. Others feature plate corals, finger corals, gorgonians or other distinct forms. Watch for manta rays, which have been sighted here on more than one occasion.

This site cannot be adequately explored in a single dive. The varied terrain and marine life encourage many divers to visit over and over again.

Large, complex arrangements of barrel sponges and crinoids typify Dangleben's Pinnacles.

17 Dangleben's North

Dangleben's North is the only reef system in the southern region that runs in an east-to-west orientation. The reef is formed by a granite extrusion from the shoreline that slopes west and north to about 80ft. The southwest edge is a nearly vertical wall dropping into the depths of the crater.

Location: South of Pointe Guignard

Depth Range: 12–100ft (4–30m)

Access: Boat

Expertise Rating: Intermediate

The mooring sits in 25ft of water and is surrounded by some superb sponge growth. The site is somewhat offshore, so it attracts larger schools of horse-eye jacks, cero mackerel and southern sennet, as well as the standard schooling reef fish. Invertebrate life is prolific, encouraged by the reef's numerous nooks and crannies. The slopes of the reef are covered by large deep-sea gorgonians and other larger sessile invertebrates.

Yellow tube sponges in deep water tend to be longer than those in shallow water.

18 Pointe Guignard

A small rocky headland protruding from the shoreline, Pointe Guignard is rich with marine life from the surface down the point slopes to the bottom at 85ft. Beyond this, the bottom is a sand flat that slopes gradually westward into the depths, but everything of real interest lies above 85ft.

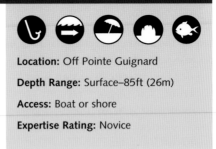

Location: Off Pointe Guignard

Depth Range: Surface–85ft (26m)

Access: Boat or shore

Expertise Rating: Novice

This site is exceptionally good for snorkeling—you can enjoy the explosion of color and activity near the surface and get a glimpse into the deeper territory, while avoiding the vertigo-inducing deep blue. The boat mooring sits south of the point in about 15ft of water. The site is accessible from shore but the walk down the cliff to the shoreline is rather long.

Virtually every surface inch of the point's rocky substrate is covered with some form of life. Encrusting sponges and corals, sea anemones, black coral as shallow as 25ft and tons of small tropicals create a fascinating community. Seahorses and frogfish are commonly found, as are lobster, crab and other creatures hiding in the many cracks and crevices.

One point of interest for divers is a narrow wave-cut cavern through the point at about 18ft. Inside the cut, which is 45ft long, check the ceiling and under the ledges for slipper lobster. Also of interest is another small cavern, which is home to a school of glassy sweepers. This cavern can be silty, so you should only venture into it if you have a fine command of buoyancy.

Hosting a wide variety of marine life, the cavern at Pointe Guignard offers many excellent photographic opportunities.

19 Champagne

This mostly shallow site is ideal for either scuba or snorkel exploration. It is named for the stream of bubbles that rises from a submerged volcanic gas vent called a fumarole. The ocean floor surrounding the small vent is stained a rust color due to the high mineral content of the gases.

Location: North of Pointe Guignard

Depth Range: 5–90ft (2–27m)

Access: Boat or shore

Expertise Rating: Novice

The site has three moorings: The northernmost lies at 10ft, the middle at 21ft and the southernmost at 30ft. Champagne can be accessed by boat or from the rocky shoreline, but parking can be somewhat limited.

While the gas vent itself is interesting, the site's biggest draw is the life around it. This is a great place to see juveniles and adults of many species. Juvenile lobster and schooling fish, as well as a large assortment of smaller tropicals, are commonly seen here. Also, some sponge and coral growth sprouts from the hard substrate beneath the thin layer of sand.

Another point of interest is a wreck site just off Champagne, which dive operators have only recently begun to visit. Two wrecks, one metal and one wooden, lie adjacent to one another at 60–95ft. The metal wreck has been there for many years and is broken into several pieces. In 1994 the *Debbie Flo*, a wooden vessel confiscated for smuggling, was sunk at the site. Large sponges, curtains of soft corals and big barracuda are just some examples of marine life found around the wrecks.

Juvenile highhats have extra-long dorsal fins.

Dominica's volcanic Dom Perignon.

Mid-Island Dive Sites

Small village communities are scattered along the west coast.

In the mid-island region, you will find more traditional Caribbean coral structures than in the other regions. Spreading patch reefs lead to steep slopes and vertical walls. With deep water nearby, the wall structures attract some blue-water pelagics but the focus is really on the wealth of tropicals, midwater schooling fish, larger predators such as amberjack and barracuda and an array of normally rare frogfish, batfish and seahorses.

The mid-island marine life is as varied as in the north and south and there are excellent coral wall structures. That said, the mid-island topography is not as unique, making the dives less challenging than in the north and south.

Mid-Island Dive Sites

	Good Snorkeling	Novice	Intermediate	Advanced
20 Canefield Tug			●	
21 Rodney's Rock	●	●		
22 Maggie's Point	●	●		
23 Castaways Reef		●		
24 Barry's Dream			●	
25 Lauro Reef			●	
26 Brain Coral Reef			●	
27 Nose Reef			●	
28 Whale Shark Reef			●	
29 Rena's Hole	●	●		
30 Coral Gardens North	●		●	

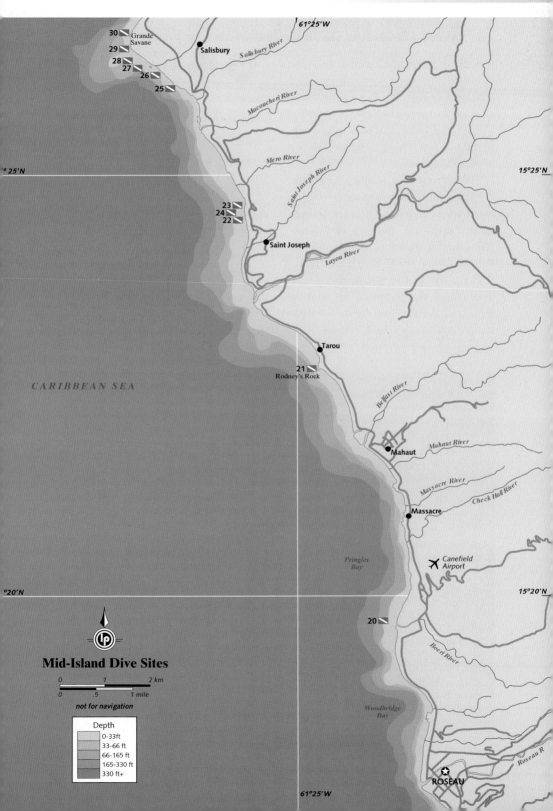

61º25'W

30 Grande
Savane
29
28
27
26
25

● Salisbury

Salisbury River

Macoucheri River

Mero River

Saint Joseph River

º 25'N   15º25'N

23
24
22

● Saint Joseph

Layou River

● Tarou

21
Rodney's Rock

Belfast River

CARIBBEAN SEA

● Mahaut

Mahaut River

Massacre River

Check Hall River

● Massacre

✈ Canefield
Airport

Pringles
Bay

º20'N   15º20'N

20

Boeri River

Mid-Island Dive Sites

0   1   2 km
0   .5   1 mile
not for navigation

Depth
0-33ft
33-66 ft
66-165 ft
165-330 ft
330 ft+

Woodbridge
Bay

Roseau R

☆
ROSEAU

61º25'W

20 | Canefield Tug

A victim of Hurricane David in 1979, the Canefield tug sunk, was refloated and attached to a mooring. But it slowly took on water and slipped below the waves for a final time. Today, this 60ft tugboat sits upright in 90ft, rising to 55ft at the top of the wheelhouse.

Location: West of the Boeri River

Depth Range: 55–90ft (17–27m)

Access: Boat

Expertise Rating: Intermediate

The bottom here is silty because the normal runoff from a nearby river is made worse by runoff from a cement factory upstream. Because of the low visibility, the wreck is dived only on Sundays, when the factory is closed.

Fortunately, the siltation has not diminished the potential for marine growth on the site. Soft corals—including gorgonians, sponges, telesto corals and more—are draped around the entire structure. The base encrustation consists of colorful corals and coralline algae. You'll likely find seahorses with their tails wrapped around gorgonians, stingrays in the silty bottom and tarpon lurking in the surface waters. The structure of the wreck itself is unstable, so penetration is unsafe and is not allowed.

Battling silty conditions, a diver examines the invertebrate life on the Canefield tug remains.

21 Rodney's Rock

South of the town of Tarou, this dive site is found just off Tarou Point, known as Rodney's Rock, which is thought to be a volcanic cap. The reef surrounding the point consists of low-lying coral formations, soft corals and sponges.

The site's main attraction, however, is the smaller marine life. A juvenile nursery sporting an amazing variety of species, it is an ideal site for both snorkelers and divers.

Batfish have been seen here, as have flying gurnards, southern stingrays, lobster, varieties of shrimp and nudibranchs and a wealth of other critters. Rodney's Rock also holds the island's record for seahorse sightings—11 were once found in a single dive. Be sure to

Location: South of the Layou River, off Rodney's Rock

Depth Range: Surface–48ft (15m)

Access: Boat or shore

Expertise Rating: Novice

take time to investigate under loose stones and look in the sand for exceptionally small juveniles.

A mated pair of flying gurnards.

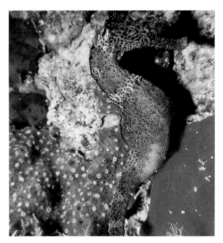

Seahorses are often found at Rodney's Rock.

The Battle that Never Was

Rodney's Rock is named for the most famous nonbattle in the history of Dominica. In the early 1800s, the English and the French engaged in a lengthy conflict over control of Dominica. One night, a lookout at Fort Cashacrou spotted French ships approaching from Martinique for a sneak attack. When Captain Rodney of the British Royal Navy heard the warning, he was on land and did not have a ship available.

This did not, however, deter the clever captain from putting forth his best effort. Rodney instructed his men to outfit the rocky Tarou Point with lamps and equipment, making it appear from a distance to be a British man-of-war. The ruse worked—the French retreated and Captain Rodney was promoted to admiral for his ingenious solution to this battle that never was.

22 Maggie's Point

Maggie's Point is a series of coral lines largely made up of pencil and finger corals beginning several hundred yards offshore and projecting toward the west. These coral spurs, which are separated by sand gullies, are dressed with azure vase sponges and crinoids.

Location: North of the Layou River, off Castaways Hotel

Depth Range: 18–90ft (6–27m)

Access: Boat

Expertise Rating: Novice

Though the formation of the reef is not especially interesting, the reef supports an impressive amount of fish life. Schools of creole wrasse, goatfish, scorpionfish, French angelfish, jackknife fish and spotted drums are commonly seen here; you'll see both juveniles and adults of each species. Maggie's Point is also the mid-island site where you are most likely to find sea turtles, usually green or hawksbill turtles.

Jackknife fish juveniles have a bar on the nose.

Beware of the venomous scorpionfish.

23 Castaways Reef

Castaways Reef is notable for the many large barrel sponges scattered across its face. This is not a deep dive: Portions of the reef are as shallow as 18ft and it reaches a maximum depth of only about 80ft. Most of the best material is found in the shallow depths.

Location: North of the Layou River, off Castaways Hotel

Depth Range: 18–80ft (6–24m)

Access: Boat

Expertise Rating: Novice

Castaways Reef is a segmented patch reef with coral heads separated by sand patches. There are blocks of eight-ray finger corals (considered unusual), which are home to groups of channel-clinging crabs. Triggerfish, barracuda, creole wrasse and parrotfish are commonly found. In sandy areas east of the reef you will usually find southern stingrays resting and feeding. Also check the sandy areas for gobies and wrasse hiding under the edges of the coral heads.

Crinoids and azure vase sponges compete for a diver's attention at Maggie's Point.

24 Barry's Dream

Barry's Dream has a nice wall that drops from about 60ft to another sloping wall at 120ft. These depths vary along the length of the wall. The south part starts at 60ft; farther north, the top of the wall is deeper, around 90ft. The best approach is to descend the mooring line to 45ft, proceed to the wall and drop to the depth you choose. From there, move north along the face of the wall and ascend to 90ft, then reverse direction and continue along the wall, ascending until you reach your starting point.

The face of the shallow wall is decorated with sponges, gorgonians and excellent hard coral formations. Several small pinnacles near the wall reach up

Location: West of Castaways Hotel, north of the Layou River

Depth Range: 42–120ft (12–36m)

Access: Boat

Expertise Rating: Intermediate

to about 80ft, and the wall itself has some nice buttresses sticking out. As always, the deeper water nearby offers the chance to see larger fish passing by. If nothing materializes there, the wall teems with enough marine life to keep you interested.

25 Lauro Reef

Though close to shore, Lauro Reef manages to gain depth quickly. You start the dive in as little as 30ft. From there, the wall drops quickly to 120ft before the reef levels off and gently slopes into deeper water.

Location: Southeast of Grande Savane

Depth Range: 30–120ft (9–36m)

Access: Boat

Expertise Rating: Intermediate

A slight overhang at 90ft protects the opening to a shallow cavern. This cavern is too small for divers to enter safely, but large enough to shelter surprises like crab, lobster and large fish. Resist the temptation to enter the cavern—you will only damage the delicate invertebrate life that drapes the entrance.

Forests of gorgonians hang from the wall, as do some large barrel sponges and boulder star corals. The fish here include pufferfish, burrfish, parrotfish, trunkfish, filefish and barracuda.

A filefish's attempt at concealment.

26 Brain Coral Reef

A dive at Brain Coral Reef begins at the mooring in 36ft. From here, a gentle slope descends to the edge of a steep wall, which drops to 130ft and beyond. Hard corals

Location: Southeast of Grande Savane

Depth Range: 35–130ft (11–40m)

Access: Boat

Expertise Rating: Intermediate

dominate the reef, which is named for the many massive brain coral heads scattered across it. Boulder star coral—in a morphotype commonly referred to as plate or sheet coral—overlap each other along the steep slope. You will also find some finger corals in the shallower areas.

Along the wall, overlapping plate corals are crowned by crinoids.

Look for lobster and channel-clinging crab and check for slipper lobster hanging upside down under the plate corals. Look for schooling chromis, sergeant major and creole wrasse. You may also see barracuda around the wall and southern stingrays resting between the coral heads at the top of the reef.

27　Nose Reef

Nose Reef is named for two unmistakable proboscular protrusions sticking out from the face of the wall. In other words, the wall has a couple of rock buttresses that look like huge honkers. The larger is found at 60ft, the smaller at 108ft. The face of the wall is a steep slope featuring lush curtains of deep-sea gorgonians combined with tube, rope and barrel sponges.

As with many of the mid-island sites, bottom dwellers such as nurse sharks and stingrays are more commonly found here than at the southern dive

Location: South of Grande Savane

Depth Range: 25–120ft (8–36m)

Access: Boat

Expertise Rating: Intermediate

sites. Seasonally, thick schools of silversides blanket the wall's face, seeking shelter among the soft coral and sponge growths. Currents can be strong along the face of the wall.

Golden crinoids extend from a brilliant vase sponge.

28 Whale Shark Reef

Whale Shark Reef sits about 1,500ft offshore and features a small wall, which drops to a larger sloping wall. You begin the dive at 45ft and then drop to about 75ft where the slope begins. The top of the reef features lush soft coral growth with a forest of deep-water gorgonians.

Location: Southwest of Grande Savane

Depth Range: 45–130ft (14–40m)

Access: Boat

Expertise Rating: Intermediate

Though the site is named for a whale shark encounter, this should be considered rare. That said, the site is well offshore, so you may see larger pelagics such as spotted eagle rays, amberjacks and rainbow runners. Great barracuda are common along the face of the wall. Start your dive deep and ascend up the smaller wall. End it by watching yellow-head jawfish found along the flats at the top of the wall.

Yellowhead jawfish hover above their burrows.

29 Rena's Hole

Rena's Hole lies directly off Grand Savane, just southwest of Coral Gardens North. This site features a classic Caribbean reef with nicely formed coral overgrowth and areas of pale sand—a relatively rare commodity on this volcanic island. Reef depths range from 25ft to a maximum of 60ft.

Location: Southwest of Grande Savane

Depth Range: 25–60ft (8–18m)

Access: Boat

Expertise Rating: Novice

A diver explores the cavern at Rena's Hole.

The site's name refers to a fairly large tunnel beneath a rocky outcropping. This "hole" is named for Rena—the girlfriend of the former divemaster who first discovered it—and is adorned with many types of colorful encrusting growth and some yellow tube and webbed sponges. Typical fish life at the site includes angelfish, sergeant major, barracuda and schooling chromis. Look out for turtles and southern stingrays in the open water and the occasional nurse shark hiding under a ledge.

30 Coral Gardens North

Coral Gardens North is found off Grand Savane, a gently sloping coastal foothill that was created from lava flows from Morne Trois Pitons. It is typical of the central areas of western Dominica.

This is an easy and satisfying dive, more like a standard Caribbean-style dive than most Dominican sites. The reef starts as shallow as 10ft and falls away at a gentle angle, which reflects the on-land topography of Grande Savane. The maximum depth is 120ft, but the variety of depths makes it a suitable site for both divers and snorkelers.

Divers use a central pinnacle to orient themselves at the beginning and the end

Location: North of Grande Savane

Depth Range: 10–120ft (3–36m)

Access: Boat

Expertise Rating: Intermediate

of the dive. The reef is somewhat hill-shaped and is very easy to navigate. Soft corals dominate the shallower depths, gradually giving way to reef-building hard corals in the deeper areas. Fields of wire coral are a striking feature. Clouds of blue and brown chromis fill the midwater region. You will also see various types of jacks, an occasional tuna and quite a few yellowtail snapper. Typical invertebrates, including shrimp and lobster, are easy to find.

Banded coral shrimp clean fish of parasites and bacteria.

An eager yellowtail snapper.

Dominica's waters are notable for the size and variety of sponges.

Northern Dive Sites

A diver examines a large purple tube sponge.

The northern region offers a combination of typical Caribbean coral reefs and sites with obvious volcanic origins. In some spots, submerged fumaroles release streams of bubbles from pockets of gas trapped under the sand. Around the Cabrits Peninsula, formed from a pair of extinct volcanoes, evidence of lava flows is etched in the steep walls.

Reefs in the Cabrits area are the result of landslides that threw piles of rocks and boulders into the sea. Over time, these boulders have become encrusted with corals and other invertebrates, attracting many varieties of fish. Farther to the north, the area returns to more traditional forms of Caribbean coral growth before emerging into the challenging diving conditions of the Guadaloupe Channel.

Northern Dive Sites

	Good Snorkeling	Novice	Intermediate	Advanced
31 Ffutsatola Reef			●	
32 Sulphur Springs & Bubbles	●		●	
33 Pia	●	●		
34 Shark's Mouth	●		●	
35 Anchor Point	●		●	
36 One-Finger Rock	●		●	
37 Five-Finger Rock	●		●	
38 Douglas Bay Point	●	●		
39 Toucari Bay Point	●		●	
40 Toucari Caves	●		●	
41 Point Break				●

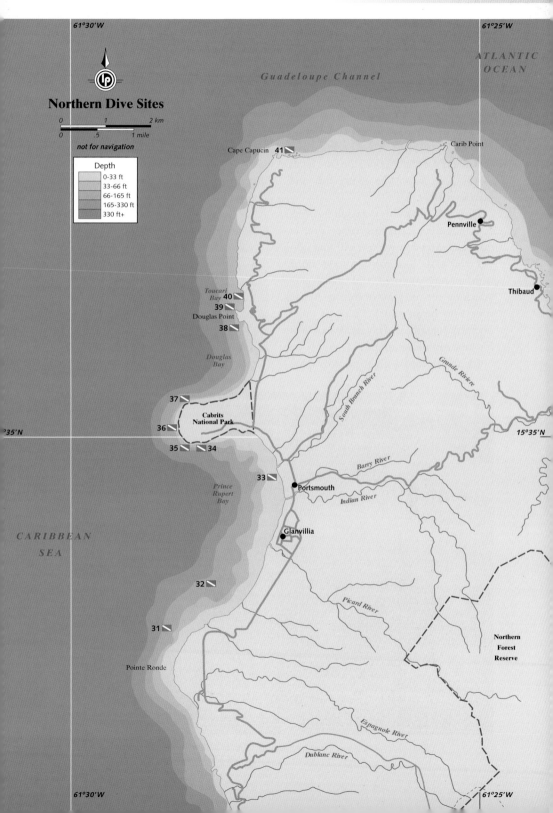

61°30'W

61°25'W

ATLANTIC OCEAN

Guadeloupe Channel

Northern Dive Sites

0   1   2 km
0   .5   1 mile

not for navigation

Depth
0-33 ft
33-66 ft
66-165 ft
165-330 ft
330 ft+

Cape Capucin **41**

Carib Point

Pennville

Thibaud

Toucari Bay **40**
39
Douglas Point
38

Douglas Bay

Grande Rivière

South Branch River

37

Cabrits National Park

36

°35'N

15°35'N

35   **34**

33

Barry River

● **Portsmouth**

Indian River

Prince Rupert Bay

● **Glanvillia**

CARIBBEAN SEA

32

Picard River

31

Pointe Ronde

Northern Forest Reserve

Espagnole River

Dublanc River

61°30'W

61°25'W

31 Ffutsatola Reef

To learn the secret of this reef, read the name backward. It offers precisely what the name says: "a lot a stuff," a small treasure trove of life. Ffutsatola is part of an infrequently visited reef complex in Prince Rupert Bay. Though the coral growth on the reef is good, the true focus of the dive is on the many fish and marine critters.

Location: North of Pointe Ronde

Depth Range: 50–90ft (15–27m)

Access: Boat

Expertise Rating: Intermediate

During the day, this is a good fish-rich dive, but the reef really comes alive at dusk and after sunset. You will find lobster and crab foraging for food along with moray, sharptail and snake eels. Watch for the red glow of shrimp eyes in your light beam and for tons of other nocturnal creatures. This reef is excellent for macrophotographers. There is so much to see that a night photographer bringing only one camera or one roll of film is bound to be disappointed.

The rare broadbanded moray forages for food.

When disturbed, the spiny lobster rapidly retreats backward into its hole.

32 Sulphur Springs & Bubbles

This area encompasses several different dive sites within the southern portion of Prince Rupert Bay—the ones you visit will depend on where you choose to dive. The reef system occupies an area more than a mile long. Depths vary greatly—some parts are at just 20ft, while others lie below sport-diving limits. The site has no moorings, so boat operators usually anchor in the deepest portion to avoid reef damage. Surface swims to the various sites—not always short but certainly manageable—are the rule.

Sulphur Springs and Bubbles are two of the better spots in the area. As their

Location: South side of Prince Rupert Bay

Depth Range: 20–120ft (6–36m)

Access: Boat

Expertise Rating: Intermediate

names suggest, both of the sites lie above gas vents that release streams of tiny bubbles from the volcanic floor. Sulphur Springs is the deeper of the two dives—you begin at 120ft and ascend a very gradual slope. Bubbles lies between 60 and 80ft. Here, the gas-vent activity tends to be somewhat more pronounced than at Sulphur Springs.

The coral profiles vary throughout the area but generally offer excellent relief with ledges and undercuts encrusted with colorful sponges and corals. Deeper portions of the reef system sport forests of wire coral. Fish life is excellent—search the bottom for jawfish and watch for huge numbers of tropicals such as basslets, wrasse, butterflyfish, angelfish and more.

A diver is dwarfed by a large barrel sponge.

Look for colorful fish like the fairy basslet.

33 *Pia*

The wreck of the *Pia* rests inside the Portsmouth Harbor, just off the Portsmouth market square. Although the wreck site is an easy swim from shore, it is rather difficult to get from the shore into the water, so approaching by boat is recommended.

A small tug not more than 60ft in length, the *Pia* offers both divers and snorkelers an opportunity to enjoy a safe first experience on a submerged wreck. Snorkelers should be especially careful of boat traffic in the area.

The wreck lies on a silty bed of sand and sea grass. Though it sits in just 6ft, the hull is partially buried. If you penetrate the engine room, however, you will find yourself in 21ft. Because of these shallow depths and the variety of life found on the wreck, the *Pia* is perfect for training and is an easy place to learn the basics of wreck penetration.

There is enough fish life here to make it satisfying dive even for an experienced diver. You will primarily find juveniles here—look for squirrelfish and schooling Caesar, blue-striped and French grunts and other tropicals.

Location: Off Portsmouth's market square

Depth Range: 6–20ft (2–6m)

Access: Boat or shore

Expertise Rating: Novice

Macrophotographers will go crazy with delight. Excellent subjects include fan worms, fileclams, tunicates (both individual and colonies), encrusting sponges, various hydroids, bristle worms, nudibranchs, flatworms, loads of small hard coral colonies and more—all in just 6ft of water!

Wreck Diving

Wreck diving can be safe and fascinating, but penetration of shipwrecks is a skiilled specialty that should not be attempted without proper training. Some of Dominica's wrecks are unstable or silty. It's best to explore the wreck's marine communities with an experienced guide.

Filter feeders, like this fileclam, thrive in Dominica's nutrient-rich waters.

34 Shark's Mouth

Shark's Mouth is the southernmost of the Cabrits sites. A pair of dormant volcanic cones (the Cabrits) form a peninsula on the north edge of Prince Rupert Bay. Landslides from the cones dropped boulders into the sea, creating an underwater Japanese garden where rocks lean against each other in a precarious balance.

Location: 150ft (45m) south of Cabrits Peninsula, west of the cruise ship dock

Depth Range: 5–120ft (2–36m)

Access: Boat or shore

Expertise Rating: Intermediate

To access the site from the southern shore, walk west from the cruise ship dock and customs house. Bring sturdy shoes as the shoreline is covered with stones and you will have to negotiate a few large rock piles. Be especially cautious of your footing during your entries and exits—not all areas are suitable.

A wealth of life has found a secure home on the stones. Sponges and hard coral formations dominate. Fully extended crinoids, a common feature of Dominican diving, comb the water for the planktonic life upon which they feed. If favorable conditions continue, over time this encrusting life will transform the network of interconnected boulders into an established biological coral reef.

Depths range from less than 10ft at the shoreline to around 120ft—shallow boulders are as richly encrusted as the deeper ones, but with different life forms. Fish life is varied and less timid than at many other sites. Since much of the site is shallow, it is perfect for snorkeling and is an ideal location for a safety stop at the end of a deep dive.

For the record, sharks are rarely found at Shark's Mouth. The name comes from a large barrel sponge with a convoluted opening that resembles a shark's open mouth. This threatening appearance is the result of the site's gentle but persistent currents.

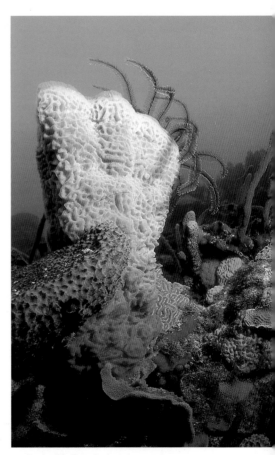

A crinoid clings to an azure vase sponge, which in turn clings to a boulder.

35 Anchor Point

Just west of the Cabrits, Anchor Point also displays the local profile of tumbled boulders encrusted with invertebrate life. Yellow tube sponges, azure vase sponges, small barrel sponges and brown tube sponges in an antler-shaped pattern are just a few examples. Crinoids of varying shades are also prolific. The slope here is not as severe as it is at Shark's Mouth. The site is appropriate for snorkelers as the shallow areas have plenty of marine life.

Shore access is limited to determined snorkelers with good footwear. The

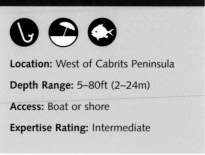

Location: West of Cabrits Peninsula

Depth Range: 5–80ft (2–24m)

Access: Boat or shore

Expertise Rating: Intermediate

shoreline is rough and the piles of rock are a bit trying to climb over. Shore diving is illegal without a registered instructor, and in any case isn't worth the effort it would require.

36 One-Finger Rock

West of the Cabrits, One-Finger Rock is named for a single rock on the shoreline. Don't bother trying to look for the rock—it's a nondescript boulder barely 2ft tall. The underwater profile mimics other dive sites in the Cabrits area, though the subsea rocks tend to be somewhat smaller and more sparse. Also, the slope of the reef here is much less severe than at other Cabrits sites.

Location: West of Cabrits Peninsula

Depth Range: 5–70ft (2–21m)

Access: Boat

Expertise Rating: Intermediate

Though it is possible to reach deeper water, there is little reason to go for a deep drop, as there is plenty to observe in the shallower water. Schooling creole wrasse are common in the midwater, sharing the space with Dominica's ubiquitous brown and blue chromis. Watch for cero, bar jack or rainbow runners cruising in from the deep water to prey on smaller fish.

One-Finger Rock is rich with invertebrate and fish life.

Sponges and a young pillar coral cover granite boulders thrown from ancient volcanoes.

37 Five-Finger Rock

Five-Finger Rock lies north of the Cabrits, directly offshore from a group of five rocks. This reef is also made up of groups of boulders that tumbled into the sea, but the slope here is much more severe than at One-Finger Rock. This site sometimes has a slight current: not too severe for most divers, but enough that filter-feeders like sponges and soft corals tend to grow to larger sizes.

Location: Northwest of Cabrits Peninsula

Depth Range: 5–80ft (2–24m)

Access: Boat

Expertise Rating: Intermediate

Five-Finger Rock displays the same wealth of marine life found on the other Cabrits sites, but has a more vertical profile to play with. As with any site exposed to deep waters, keep an eye on the open water for larger fish. Don't forget to look for smaller critters concealing themselves under the edges of the boulders.

38 Douglas Bay Point

Douglas Bay Point hits the water and drops down to around 90ft. The slope is richly coated with life starting almost at the water line. Several large boulders create small but penetrable archways that shelter a wide variety of creatures. This site is similar to Toucari Bay Point to the north, but offers more topographical interest.

Location: North side of Douglas Bay, southwest of Douglas Point

Depth Range: 5–60ft (2–18m)

Access: Boat or shore

Expertise Rating: Novice

Though shore access is possible, it requires a taxing hike and a clamber over rocks and brush. Solo diving is not permitted and is difficult besides. It is best to use a dive boat. Snorkeling here is good because, like many of the northern sites, the shallow rocky foreground is a perfect substrate for growing invertebrate life. Shore snorkeling is a practical alternative only for the fit and adventurous. Be very cautious upon entry and exit.

The marine life here is typical of the area—crinoids, sponges, shrimp, smaller tropicals, schooling chromis and creole wrasse are common. One unusual item is the purple tube sponge, clusters of which are found here and at other locations to the north.

An arrow crab rests on a golden crinoid.

Northern sites host the unusual purple tube sponge.

39 Toucari Bay Point

Toucari Bay Point sits off the southern shore of Toucari Bay. Much like Douglas Bay Point to the south, the point slopes gradually from the surface down to the floor of the bay.

Location: South side of Toucari Bay, north of Douglas Point

Depth Range: Surface–100ft (30m)

Access: Boat or shore

Expertise Rating: Intermediate

The topography and the marine inhabitants are similar at the two spots. There are fine examples of invertebrate growth including sponges, soft corals, gorgonians and small sprouts of black coral. Fish life here mimics much of the surrounding area, with more angelfish than at other sites. Here, too, the underwater growth begins very close to the surface, so snorkeling is an excellent option.

Wind direction and water conditions permitting, Toucari Bay Point is another accessible shore snorkel. Unfortunately, the climb down from the road is not easy and the swim from shore is rather long; be certain you are up to a challenge. Boat excursions are an easier option, and this dive is often combined with a Toucari Caves dive.

40 Toucari Caves

In the heart of Toucari Bay, the Toucari caves sit offshore in just 40ft, with the top of the reef at 15ft. The shallow depth makes it ideal for free-divers. This site can be accessed by boat or from the shore, though it is a bit of a swim. It can be tricky to locate the caves themselves, so it is best to visit with a local dive operator.

Location: In Toucari Bay, 300ft (90m) offshore

Depth Range: 15–40ft (5–12m)

Access: Boat or shore

Expertise Rating: Novice

The cave system is actually more of a small cavern system, as the honeycomb of holes interlacing the reef is short and the entrance and exit are always visible. The system is an extension of the hard substrate underlying the sandy bottom and is surrounded by a rich coral garden reaching some 70ft in depth.

Be cautious when entering the caverns—the sessile marine life is vulnerable to even the slightest touch. Growths of black coral, telesto corals and golden sea spray hang from the ceilings and sprout from the floors of the caverns. Sponge growths and other colorful invertebrates sprout from the walls. Look for Spanish lobster clinging to the cavern ceilings. Smaller Caribbean tropicals abound, but not to the exclusion of larger animals. Search the sand for southern stingrays, watch for sea turtles and keep your eyes peeled for the resident great barracuda.

Shallow caverns in Toucari Bay host an array of tropical fish and invertebrates.

41 Point Break

Diveable only on the few days a year when conditions are optimal, Point Break is the wild, unexplored northern edge of Dominican diving. Put simply, expect the unexpected. Here, Atlantic currents sweep through the channel between Dominica and Guadeloupe. As a result, the water is incredibly clear and currents are strong.

Point Break is not just one site but rather encompasses a largely unexplored area in the Guadeloupe Channel stretching east from the island's northwest corner. The wall descending into the depths of the channel is overgrown with huge corals and large rooted and mobile filter feeders. The wall varies greatly— some areas are absolutely vertical or have a steep slope, while others feature gullies and cuts or overhangs and caverns.

Consider Point Break to be very advanced diving. If you have the necessary skills and conditions are favorable, go for it. You never know what you'll find— you may see sharks, whales or dolphins, or you may be the one to discover the rumored remnants of a shipwreck.

Location: North of Cape Capucin

Depth Range: 25–130ft (8–40m)

Access: Boat

Expertise Rating: Advanced

This Caribbean reef shark is just one of many surprises you may find in the far northern region.

Crinoids, a notable feature of Dominican diving, comb the water for food.

Marine Life

The sheer number of reef fish in Dominican waters is impressive, and the island is home to relatively large populations of rare and unusual marine life. The following is a sampling of Dominica's most commonly seen fish and invertebrate marine life, including a photo, common name and scientific name (genus and species) for each. Following that, you will find photos and descriptions for potentially hazardous marine life that you may find in Dominican waters.

Common Fish

French angelfish
Pomacanthus paru

gray angelfish
Pomacanthus arcuatus

queen angelfish
Holacanthus ciliaris

banded butterflyfish
Chaetodon striatus

spotfin butterflyfish
Chaetodon ocellatus

coney
Epinephelus fulvus

yellowtail damselfish
Microspathodon chrysurus

sharptail eel
Myrichthys breviceps

spotted snake eel
Ophichthus ophis

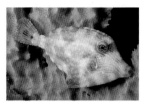

pygmy filefish
Stephenolepis setifer

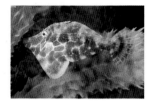

slender filefish
Monacanthus tuckeri

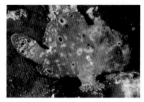

longlure frogfish
Antennarius multiocellatus

pallid goby
Coryphopterus eidolon

sharknose goby
Gobiosoma evelynae

flying gurnard
Dactylopterus volitans

barred hamlet
Hypoplectrus puella

bar jack
Caranx ruber

yellowhead jawfish
Opistognathus aurifrons

shortfin pipefish
Cosmocampus elucens

sharpnose puffer
Canthigaster rostrata

schoolmaster
Lutjanus apodus

glasseye snapper
Priancanthus cruentatus

yellowtail snapper
Ocyurus chrysurus

blackbar soldierfish
Myripristis jacobus

squirrelfish
Holocentrus ascensionis

tobaccofish
Serranus tabacarius

trumpetfish
Aulostomus maculatus

Common Invertebrates

rose lace coral
Stylaster roseus

orange ball corallimorpharian
Pseudocorynactis caribbeorum

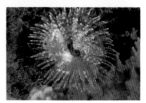

magnificent feather duster
Sabellastarte magnifica

rough fileclam
Lima scabra

flamingo tongue
Cyphoma gibbosum

spotted spiny lobster
Panulirus guttatus

amber pen shell
Pinna carnea

banded coral shrimp
Stenopus hispidus

spotted cleaner shrimp
Periclimenes yucatanicus

squat anemone shrimp
Thor amboinensis

Caribbean reef squid
Sepioteuthis sepioidea

mangrove tunicate
Ecteinascidia turbinata

Hazardous Marine Life

Marine creatures almost never attack divers, but many are well able to defend themselves if molested, whether deliberately or inadvertantly. The ability to recognize and avoid hazardous creatures is a valuable asset in avoiding accident and injury. The following are some of the potentially hazardous creatures most commonly found in Dominica.

Barracuda

Barracuda are identifiable by their long, silver, cylindrical bodies and razor-like teeth protruding out of an underslung jaw. They swim alone or in small groups, continually opening and closing their mouths to assist respiration. Though barracuda will hover near divers to observe, they are actually somewhat shy. Don't bother them and they won't bother you.

Fire Coral

Mustard-brown in color, fire coral is found in shallower waters encrusting and taking the shape of dead gorgonians or coral. It forms multiple branches that are usually smooth and cylindrical and dotted with little holes, out of which the hair-like polyps protrude. Upon contact, the small stinging cells located on the polyps discharge, causing a burning sensation that lasts for several minutes and can sometimes cause red welts on the skin. If you brush against fire coral, do not rub the affected area as you will spread the small stinging particles. Cortisone cream can reduce inflammation and minor abrasions can be treated with meat tenderizer and antibiotic cream. Serious cuts should be treated by a doctor.

Lesser Electric Ray

Approximately 15 inches long, the lesser electric ray can deliver an electric shock if touched. Originating from a point near the eyes, the shock is intended to render its prey helpless. These rays usually rest in sandy areas and are less aggressive than other electric rays. The shock, unpleasant but milder than that of other rays, does not last long and is generally not disabling.

Moray Eel

Distinguished by their long, thick, snake-like bodies and tapered heads, eels won't bother you unless you bother them. Don't feed them—eels have the unfortunate combination of sharp teeth and poor eyesight, so they cannot always distinguish between food and your hand. Likewise, don't put your hand in a dark hole, because it just might house an angry eel. If you are bitten, don't try to pull your hand away as its teeth are extraordinarily sharp. Let the eel release it and then surface slowly, apply first aid and head for the nearest hospital.

Scorpionfish

It may be one of the sea's best-camouflaged creatures, but if you are punctured by the poisonous spine hidden among its fins, you'll know you've found a scorpi-

onfish. Scorpionfish are often mistaken for rocks, but most have large appendages (cirri) or "plumes" above the eyes. Scorpionfish tend to lie on the bottom or on coral, so be sure to practice good buoyancy control and watch where you put your hands. If you get stung, get medical attention as soon as possible because stings can result in severe allergic reactions and pain and infection are almost guaranteed.

Sea Urchin

Long-spined sea urchins are abundant in the Caribbean. Look for their black bodies and long needle-like spines. The spines are the urchin's most dangerous weapon, able to penetrate neoprene wetsuits, booties and gloves with ease. The instant pain lets you know you've been jabbed. Urchins tend to live in shallow areas near shore and come out of their shelters under coral heads at night. Minor punctures can be treated by extracting the spines and treating the wound with antibiotic cream. More serious injuries should be looked at by a doctor.

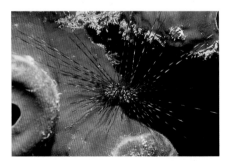

Shark

Sharks come in many shapes and sizes. They are most recognizable by their triangular dorsal fin. Sharks, perhaps more than any other marine creature, demand that divers practice common sense and respect. Sharks will generally not attack unless provoked, so don't taunt, tease or feed them. Though encountering a shark can be an exciting, mutually respectful experience, you never know when a shark might be grumpy. Any shark injury obviously calls for immediate medical attention.

In Dominica, divers often encounter nurse sharks sleeping under ledges. Some people consider them harmless because they have small teeth, but once they bite, they can be tenacious. Do not be tempted to pull their tails. Nurse-shark bites are seldom serious, but can be painful nonetheless.

Southern Stingray

Gray in color and measuring up to 5ft from wing tip to wing tip, the southern stingray has one or two sharp venomous barbs near the base of its tail. The barbs

are seldom used offensively and the majority of injuries result from people disturbing a ray resting in the sand. Rays like shallow waters and tend to rest on silty or sandy bottoms, often burying themselves in the sand. Generally, southern stingrays will allow a close approach, as long as you are gentle and slow. If disturbed, it will arch its body in preparation for flight—do not interfere at this point. Though injuries are uncommon, wounds can be severe and victims should seek medical aid immediately.

Bristle Worm

Also called fire worms, bristle worms can be found on most reefs. They have segmented bodies that are covered with either tufts or bundles of sensory hairs that extend in tiny, sharp, detachable bristles. If you touch one, the tiny stinging bristles embed in your skin and cause a

burning sensation that may be followed by a red spot or welt. The bristles will work their way out of your skin in a couple of days, though you can try to scrape them off with the edge of a knife.

Basic First-Aid Procedures

The measures described below are basic first aid using commonly available materials and equipment, and are not a substitute for medical attention. The seriousness of an encounter with a hazardous marine animal depends not only on the nature of the animal but on the location of the wound—a bite, spine or sting near the eyes should be treated differently than one to a calloused heel.

1. Immediately, in the water if possible, check that the victim is breathing. If not, clear the airway and begin mouth-to-mouth resuscitation. Remove the victim from the water as quickly as possible, check for breathing and heartbeat and begin CPR if necessary.

2. To minimize shock, place the victim in a head-down position; minimize blood loss by applying pressure and/or a tourniquet and elevate the limb involved.

3. Try to remove spicules, spines or bristles with tweezers or adhesive tape, but leave any that are deeply embedded (in joints, near eyes or near major blood vessels) for surgical removal later. Wash the area with sterile (boiled) water. If a sponge is thought to be involved, soak the area with vinegar diluted with an equal volume of sterile water. Venom and pain may be reduced by heating the afflicted area with warm water or a hot hair drier.

4. If a creature with nematocysts was involved, the sting should be washed out with sea water. (Do not use fresh water, as nematocysts will trigger in defense of something "unnatural" to them; fresh water may in fact result in additional stings.) Flood the area with diluted vinegar and remove

any visible nematocysts with a pair of tweezers. Apply shaving cream to the site, and carefully scrape it with a razor or knife. Flood the area again with diluted vinegar, followed by several teaspoons of baking soda (sodium bicarbonate) dissolved in sterile water. Make sure nematocysts are not spread to other areas—especially the eyes—or to other people.

5. Apply a topical antibiotic such as bacitracin or neomycin if available. Place a sterile dressing over the wound—a section cut from a clean cotton T-shirt or washcloth, boiled and then dried will do fine—and secure it with tape or string.

Diving Conservation & Awareness

For years, environmental awareness regarding Dominica's rainforest has been growing. Concerns about this fragile ecosystem and its endangered inhabitants brought protective measures to the island relatively early. A substantial portion of the land—including the Northern Forest Reserve, the Central Forest Reserve and Morne Trois Pitons National Park—has been set aside as national forest, where it is illegal to remove either plant or animal life.

The underwater world, however, has been slower to receive protected status, largely due to Dominica's traditional fishing practices. Fish traps are common at some dive sites, much to the dismay of visiting divers. Though they may upset you, do not disturb the traps—in the traditional fishing villages they are the lifeline of the community.

That said, great strides have been made in recent years toward protecting the underwater environment. The entire Soufriere Bay area—from Champagne around to the Atlantic side—is now a marine reserve. Some areas are designated as no-use zones, and in other areas fishing is allowed by handline only. Fish traps, gill nets and anchoring on the reef are all banned. The Cabrits area—from the cruise ship dock up the coastline past Toucari Bay—falls within the Cabrits Marine Reserve and has similar regulations. Sadly, restrictions are not always enforced. You will see violations, but the use of fish traps is diminishing and net use on the reefs is rare. All major dive sites have moorings, making anchor damage a thing of the past. Spearfishing is prohibited at all dive sites.

Responsible Diving

Dive sites tend to be located where the reefs and walls display the most beautiful corals and sponges. It only takes a moment—an inadvertently placed hand or a careless brush or kick with a fin—to destroy this fragile, living part of our delicate ecosystem. Please consider the following suggestions when diving:

1. Never drop boat anchors onto a coral reef and take care not to ground boats on coral. Encourage dive operators and regulatory bodies in their efforts to establish permanent moorings at dive sites.

2. Practice and maintain proper buoyancy control and avoid overweighting. Be aware that buoyancy can change over the period of an extended trip: initially you may breathe harder and need more weight; a few days later you may breath more easily and need less weight. Be careful about buoyancy loss: As you go deeper, your wetsuit compresses and you lose buoyancy.

3. Avoid touching living marine organisms with your body or dragging equipment across the reef. Polyps can be damaged by even the gentlest contact. Never stand on coral, even if it looks solid and robust. The use of gloves is no longer recommended: It just makes it too easy to hold on to the reef and the abrasion caused by gloves may be more damaging to the reef than your hands are. If you must hold on to the reef, touch only exposed rock or dead coral.

4. Be conscious of your fins. Even without contact, the surge from heavy fin strokes near the reef can do damage. Avoid full-leg kicks when working close to the bottom and when leaving a photo scene. When you inadvertently kick something, stop kicking! It seems obvious, but some divers either panic or are completely oblivious when they bump something. When treading water in shallow reef areas, take care not to kick up clouds of sand. Settling sand can easily smother the delicate organisms of the reef.

5. Attach all dangling gauges, computer consoles and octopus regulators to your BC. These are like miniature wrecking balls to a reef.

6. When swimming in strong currents, be especially careful about leg kicks and handholds.

7. Photographers must be extra careful. Cameras and equipment affect buoyancy. Changing f-stops, framing a subject and maintaining position for a photo often conspire to prohibit the ideal "no-touch" approach on a reef. When you must use "holdfasts," choose them intelligently (i.e., use only one finger for leverage off an area of dead coral).

8. Resist the temptation to collect or buy corals or shells. Aside from the ecological damage, taking home marine souvenirs depletes the beauty of a site and spoils the enjoyment of others.

9. Be sure to take home all your trash and any litter you may find as well. Plastics in particular are a serious threat to marine life.

10. Resist the temptation to feed fish. You may disturb their normal eating habits, encourage aggressive behavior or feed them food that is detrimental to their health.

Dive Fest

Since 1994, the Dominica Watersports Association has sponsored Dive Fest, an annual week-long series of dive-related activities. Dive Fest starts the weekend preceding July 4 and lasts until the following weekend. The event is largely educational—activities are intended to expose visitors and local children to the wonders of the underwater realm. There are slide shows, free snorkeling lessons and snorkel trips. Other activities include traditional Carib canoe races, kayak races, underwater treasure hunts and free resort courses. For the visiting diver, this is a great time to get discounts on whale-watching and dive trips.

Listings

Telephone Calls

All phone numbers in Dominica have seven digits. From North America, dial 1 + 767 (Dominica's area code) + the local number. From outside North America, use your country's international access code + 767 + the local number.

Accommodations

Anchorage Hotel
P.O. Box 34
Roseau, Dominica
☎ 448-2638 fax: 448-5680
anchorage@cwdom.dm
www.anchoragehotel.dm
Rooms: 32
Other: In Castle Comfort, 1 mile south of Roseau; bar, restaurant, swimming pool; PADI 5-Star facility

Castaways Hotel
P.O. Box 5
Roseau, Dominica
☎ 449-6244 fax: 449-6246
castaways@cwdom.dm
www.castaways.dm
Rooms: 26
Other: 2 miles north of the Layou River; 2 bars, restaurant; PADI 5-Star facility

Castle Comfort Lodge and Dive Dominica
P.O. Box 2253
Roseau, Dominica
☎ 448-2188 fax: 448-6088
dive@cwdom.dm
www.divedominica.com
Rooms: 15
Other: In Castle Comfort, 1 mile south of Roseau; restaurant, spa; PADI 5-Star facility

Coconut Beach Hotel
P.O. Box 37
Portsmouth, Dominica
☎ 445-5393 fax: 445-5693
Rooms: 22
Other: 1 mile south of Portsmouth; bar, restaurant

Evergreen Hotel
P.O. Box 309
Roseau, Dominica
evergreen@tod.dm
www.delphis.dm/evergreen.htm
☎ 448-3288 fax: 448-6800
Rooms: 16
Other: In Castle Comfort, 1 mile south of Roseau; bar, restaurant, swimming pool

Fort Young Hotel
P.O. Box 519
Roseau, Dominica
fortyoung@tod.dm
www.delphis.dm/fortyoung.htm
☎ 448-5000 fax: 448-5006
Rooms: 33
Other: At Fort Young in southern Roseau; bar, restaurant, swimming pool

Picard Beach Cottage Resort
P.O. Box 34
Roseau, Dominica
picardbeach@tod.dm
☎ 445-5131 fax: 445-5599
Rooms: 8
Other: $\frac{1}{2}$ mile south of Portsmouth; bar, restaurant, swimming pool

Portsmouth Beach Hotel
P.O. Box 34
Roseau, Dominica
pbh@tod.dm
☎ 445-5142 fax: 445-5599
Rooms: 170
Other: $\frac{1}{2}$ mile south of Portsmouth; bar, restaurant, swimming pool

Mountain Retreats

Travelers seeking a tranquil, natural alternative to coastal hotels should consider one of Dominica's several mountain retreats. The following hotels are found inland, set back in the rainforest or in the hills. Divers should be sure to ask about transportation between hotels and the dive boats. Do your research: Some dive operators offer packages with mountain retreats that include transportation. Other options include renting a car or using minivans or taxis.

Exotica
P.O. Box 109
Roseau, Dominica
☎ 448-8839 fax: 448-8829
exotica@tod.dm
www.dephis.dm/eiexotica.htm
Rooms: 8
Other: 3 miles east of Roseau on Morne Anglais; restaurant

Papillote
P.O. Box 109
Roseau, Dominica
☎ 448-2287 fax: 448-2285
papillote@tod.dm
Rooms: 8
Other: 3 miles northeast of Roseau, near Trafalgar Falls; bar, restaurant

Petit Coulibri Guest Cottages
P.O. Box 331
Roseau, Dominica
☎ 446-3150 fax: 446-3150
barnardm@tod.dm
Rooms: 5
Other: 2 miles east of Soufriere; restaurant, swimming pool

Roxy's Mountain Lodge
P.O. Box 265
Roseau, Dominica
☎ 448-4854 fax: 448-4854
bruneyr@tod.dm
Rooms: 17
Other: At the base of Morne Trois Piton, 6 miles northeast of Roseau; bar, restaurant

Diving Services

Anchorage Whale Watch & Dive Centre
P.O. Box 34
Roseau, Dominica
☎ 448-2638 fax: 448-5680
anchorage@cwdom.dm
www.anchoragehotel.dm
Sales: Yes **Rentals:** Yes
Credit Cards: All major credit cards
Boats: *Merci Bon Dieu*, 39ft Key West hull, 30 whale watchers or snorkelers, 24 divers; *Domnik*, 30ft Island Hopper, 20 whale watchers or snorkelers, 14 divers; *Fun*, 18ft Bayliner, 6 whale watchers or snorkelers; scout boat; ski boat
Trips: 9am 2-tank, night dives, snorkel trips, whale watching trips
Courses: PADI Open Water–Divemaster, some specialties
Comments: In Castle Comfort, 1 mile south of Roseau; specializes in southern and mid-island sites, though a subsidiary shop handles northern sites

Cabrits Dive Centre
Picard Estate
Portsmouth, Dominica
☎ 445-3010 fax: 445-3011
cabritsdive@cwdom.dm
www.cabritsdive.com
Sales: Yes **Rentals:** Yes
Credit Cards: Visa, MasterCard
Boats: *Down Under*, 23ft aluminum, 150hp Johnson outboard engine; *Bottom Time,* 23ft aluminum, 150hp Johnson outboard engine
Trips: 9am 2-tank, 2pm 2-tank, sunset dives (1-tank late afternoon and 1-tank night dive), night dives upon request
Courses: PADI Open Water–Assistant Instructor, 12 specialties
Comments: In Portsmouth; specializes in mid-island and northern sites

Dive Castaways
P.O. Box 5
Roseau, Dominica
☎ 449-6244 fax: 449-6246
Sales: None **Rentals:** Yes
Credit Cards: All major credit cards
Boats: *Zortola*, 28ft open fisherman with cover, 7 divers; *Cat Mon Du*, 40ft Bellecraft Catamaran, 14 divers
Trips: 9am 2-tank, afternoon and night dives upon request, whale watching
Courses: PADI Open Water–Divemaster, specialties
Comments: 2 miles north of the Layou River; specializes in mid-island sites, but dives north and south as well

**Dive Dominica and
Castle Comfort Lodge**
P.O. Box 2253
Roseau, Dominica
☎ 448-2188 fax: 448-6088
Sales: Yes **Rentals:** Yes
Credit Cards: Most major credit cards
Boats: *Yan Yan*, 30ft Island Hopper, 10 divers; *Arienne*, 36ft Bellecraft catamaran, 20 divers; *Olga*, 47ft Bellecraft catamaran, 20 divers; *Barana*, 45ft Corinthian catamaran, dedicated snorkel/whale-watch vessel, 50 snorkelers
Trips: 9am 2-tank dive, snorkel trips, whale-watching trips
Courses: PADI, NAUI, NASDS Open Water–Divemaster, 6 specialties
Comments: In Castle Comfort, 1 mile south of Roseau; specializes in southern and mid-island sites

East Carib Dive
P.O. Box 375
Roseau, Dominica
☎ 449-6575 fax: 449-6575
ecd@cwdom.dm
www.eastcaribdive.dm
Sales: None **Rentals:** Snorkel gear only
Credit Cards: Visa, MasterCard, Discover
Boats: *Shamu*, 21ft custom-built aluminum, 6 divers
Trips: 9am 2-tank dive, night dives
Courses: PADI and CMAS Open Water
Comments: 1 mile north of the Layou river, in St. Joseph; specializes in mid-island sites but dives north and south as well

Nature Island Dive
P.O. Box 2354
Roseau, Dominica
☎ 449-8181 fax: 449-8182
www.natureislanddive.dm
Sales: None **Rentals:** Snorkel gear, ocean kayaks, mountain bikes
Credit Cards: Visa, MasterCard, Discover
Boats: *Nikki*, 34ft custom-built aluminum catamaran, 16 divers; *2* 21ft custom-built aluminum, 10 divers
Trips: 9am 2-tank, 11:30am 1-tank/snorkeling, afternoon and night dives upon request
Courses: PADI Open Water–Divemaster, 11 specialties
Comments: In Soufriere; specializes in southern sites

Tourist Offices

Dominica Division of Tourism
National Development Council
P.O. Box 293
Roseau, Dominica
☎ 448-2045 fax: 448-5840

Canada
OECS Mission in Canada
112 Kent St., Suite 1050
Ottawa, Ontario KIP 5P2, Canada
☎ 613-236-8952 fax: 613-236-3042

United Kingdom
Caribbean Tourism Organization
Vigilant House
120 Wilton Rd., Suite 315
Victoria, London SW1V 1JZ, UK
☎ 0-171-233-8382 fax: 0-171-873-8551

United States
Dominica Tourist Office
10 East 21st St., Suite 600
New York, NY 10010, USA
☎ 212-475-7542 fax: 212-475-9728

Index

dive sites covered in this book appear in **bold** type

Lonely Planet Series Descriptions

Lonely Planet **travel guides** explore a destination in depth with options to suit a range of budgets. With reliable, practical advice on getting around, restaurants and accommodations, these easy-to-use guides also include detailed maps, color photographs, extensive background material and coverage of sites both on and off the beaten track.

For budget travelers **shoestring guides** are the best single source of travel information covering an entire continent or large region. Written by experienced travelers these 'tried and true' classics offer reliable, first-hand advice on transportation, restaurants and accommodations, and insider tips for avoiding bureaucratic confusion and stretching money as far as possible.

City guides cover many of the world's great cities with full-color photographs throughout, front and back cover gatefold maps, and information for every traveler's budget and style. With information for business travelers, all the best places to eat and shop and itinerary suggestions for long and short-term visitors, city guides are a complete package.

Lonely Planet **phrasebooks** have essential words and phrases to help travelers communicate with the locals. With color tabs for quick reference, an extensive vocabulary, use of local scripts and easy-to-follow pronunciation instructions, these handy, pocket-sized language guides cover most situations a traveler is likely to encounter.

Lonely Planet **walking guides** cover some of the world's most exciting trails. With detailed route descriptions including degrees of difficulty and best times to go, reliable maps and extensive background information, these guides are an invaluable resource for both independent hikers and those in organized groups.

Lonely Planet **travel atlases** are thoroughly researched and fact-checked by the guidebook authors to ensure they complement the books. And the handy format means none of the holes, wrinkles, tears, or constant folding and refolding of flat maps. They include background information in five languages.

Journeys is a new series of travel literature that captures the spirit of a place, illuminates a culture, recounts an adventure and introduces a fascinating way of life. Written by a diverse group of writers, they are tales to read while on the road or at home in your favorite armchair.

Entertaining, independent and adventurous, Lonely Planet **videos** encourage the same approach to travel as the guidebooks. Currently broadcast throughout the world, this award-winning series features all original footage and music.

Lonely Planet Pisces Books

The **Diving & Snorkeling** books are dive guides to top destinations worldwide. Beautifully illustrated with full-color photos throughout, the series explores the best diving and snorkeling areas and prepares divers for what to expect when they get there. Each site is described in detail, with information on suggested ability levels, depth, visibility, and, of course, marine life. There's basic topside information as well for each destination. Don't miss the guides to:

Australia's Great Barrier Reef

Australia: Southeast Coast

Bahamas: Family Islands
  & Grand

Bahamas: Nassau &
  New Providence

Baja California

Bali & the Komodo Region

Belize

Bermuda

Best Caribbean Diving

Bonaire

British Virgin Islands

Cayman Islands

Cocos Island

Cozumel

Cuba

Curaçao

Fiji

Florida Keys

Guam & Yap

Hawaiian Islands

Jamaica

Northern California &
  Monterey Peninsula

Pacific Northwest

Palau

Papua New Guinea

Puerto Rico

Red Sea

Roatan & Honduras'
  Bay Islands

Scotland

Seychelles

Southern California

St. Maarten, Saba,
  & St. Eustatius

Texas

Truk Lagoon

Turks & Caicos

U.S. Virgin Islands

Vanuatu

Plus illustrated natural history guides:

Pisces Guide to Caribbean Reef Ecology

Great Reefs of the World

Sharks of Tropical & Temperate Seas

Venomous & Toxic Marine Life of the World

Watching Fishes

Lonely Planet Online

Get the latest travel information before you leave or while you're on the road

Whether you've just begun planning your next trip, or you're chasing down specific info on currency regulations or visa requirements, check out Lonely Planet Online for up-to-the-minute travel information.

As well as travel profiles of your favorite destinations (including maps and photos), you'll find current reports from our researchers and other travelers, updates on health and visas, travel advisories, and discussion of the ecological and political issues you need to be aware of as you travel.

There's also an online travelers' forum where you can share your experience of life on the road, meet travel companions and ask other travelers for their recommendations and advice. We also have plenty of links to other online sites useful to independent travelers.

And of course we have a complete and up-to-date list of all Lonely Planet travel products including guides, phrasebooks, atlases, Journeys and videos and a simple online ordering facility if you can't find the book you want elsewhere.

www.lonelyplanet.com or **AOL keyword: lp**

Travel news goes off faster than a bag of prawns in the sun.

Lonely Planet's new monthly email newsletter, **Comet**, brings you the latest travel news, destination ideas, travel tips, health advice, travellers' yarns, raging debates and competitions. All this, and it's free.

To subscribe just enter your email at:
http://www.lonelyplanet.com/comet/

Where to Find Us . . .

Lonely Planet is known worldwide for publishing practical, reliable and no-nonsense travel information in our guides and on our web site. The Lonely Planet list covers just about every accessible part of the world. Currently there are nine series: *Pisces books, travel guides, shoestring guides, walking guides, city guides, phrasebooks, audio packs, travel atlases* and *Journeys*–a unique collection of travel writing.

Lonely Planet Publications

Australia
PO Box 617, Hawthorn 3122, Victoria
☎ (03) 9819 1877 fax (03) 9819 6459
e-mail talk2us@lonelyplanet.com.au

USA
150 Linden Street
Oakland, California 94607
☎ (510) 893 8555, (800) 275 8555
fax (510) 893 8563
e-mail info@lonelyplanet.com

UK
10A Spring Place,
London NW5 3BH
☎ (0171) 428 4800 fax (0171) 428 4828
e-mail go@lonelyplanet.co.uk

France
1 rue du Dahomey
75011 Paris
☎ 01 55 25 33 00 fax 01 55 25 33 01
e-mail bip@lonelyplanet.fr

World Wide Web: www.lonelyplanet.com or **AOL keyword: lp**